A DECEPTIVE Orthodoxy

Fred DeRuvo

STUDY • GROW • KNOW
It's always time to study, grow and know your faith!

www.studygrowknow.com

Published in Scotts Valley, California, by Study-Grow-Know
www.studygrowknow.com • www.rightly-dividing.com

Cover design by Fred DeRuvo, for Study-Grow-Know

Library of Congress Cataloging-in-Publication Data

DeRuvo, Fred, 1957 –

ISBN 0982644310
EAN-13 9780982644317

1. Religion – Christian Theology - Eschatology

Contents

Do not answer a fool according to his folly,

lest you yourself also be like him.

– Proverbs 26:4 (NET)

FOREWORD

It has come to my attention that not everyone believes the PreTrib Rapture doctrine is viable. Can you believe that? Here I was going along, minding my own business when this news slaps me across the face. Unbelievable. Not only this, but also some people actually believe that the PreTrib Rapture is a *deception of the End* Times! I am *shocked*! What to do? What to do?

In all seriousness, I am well aware of the fact that not only are there individuals who do not see the PreTrib Rapture as viable, but some even consider it be blasphemous heresy! I do not mind at all if someone disagrees with my understanding of Scripture. The plain fact of the matter is that I am still growing in my faith and it is possible that I will alter some of my conclusions I currently have regarding some of the biblical doctrines. I have no intention of all of a sudden coming out and denying the virgin birth, the deity of Christ, the Triune nature of God, salvation by grace, through faith, in Christ, and things of that nature. However, where there is a bit of wiggle room, there is room to alter an opinion.

However, the more I study things, the more I find people using fabricated arguments – what some term extra-biblical arguments – to shore up their own doctrinal position. Many of these extra-biblical arguments do not stand up to *human* scrutiny, much less *biblical* scrutiny. Yet, some, in their attempts to make themselves feel loftier about their own position, continually and consistently use these arguments as a sort of badge of honor. One of the more commonly stated reasons for rejecting the PreTrib Rapture is that it is said to be a major reason for the coming apostasy. Some go so far as to say that it is *the* reason for the apostasy, which has begun to come upon the world. We will take this to its logical conclusion to see if, in actuality, the

PreTrib Rapture *is* in any way, part of the arriving apostasy, which we were warned about a bit less than 2,000 years ago.

In this book, I highlight some of the common arguments that are tossed out there in attempts to negate the biblical nature of the PreTrib Rapture position. Moreover, I cite numerous movements that are alive and well in today's visible Church, which many others and I believe to be the authentic threats to the gospel of Christ.

Will this book solve any problems? Will it cause anyone to drop his or her claims against the PreTrib Rapture position? I doubt it, because it is very common to read and/or hear statements like this: *"The PreTrib Rapture is not found anywhere in the Bible."* With people making declarative statements like that, it is no wonder that the debate continues. It would be far more accurate to say, *"I do not find reference to the PreTrib Rapture in the Bible,"* or *"I do not believe the Bible teaches a PreTrib Rapture."* These types of statements leave room for discussion. The declarative statements not only leave no room for discussion, but also simply create an atmosphere of angst.

One thing *is* certain though, and that is, that this particular author will feel much better for having written it.

Fred DeRuvo, January 2010

Chapter 1

Living in the Land of Myopia

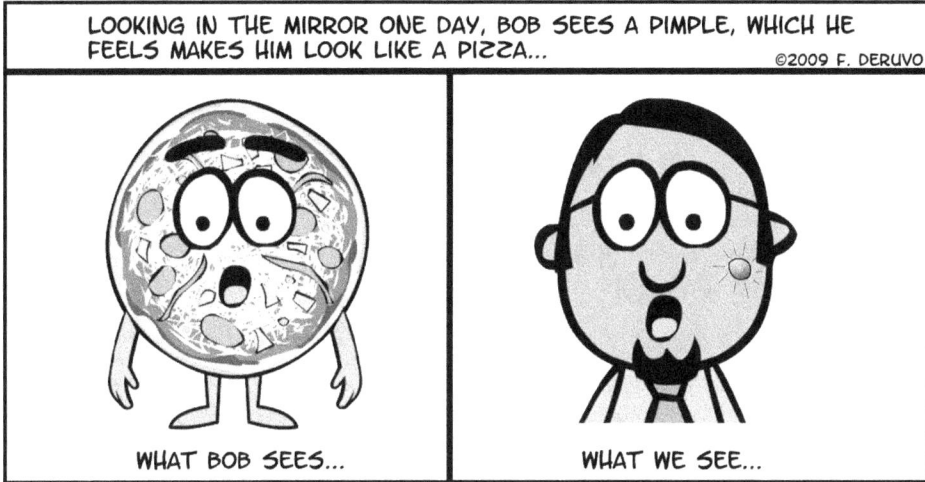

LOOKING IN THE MIRROR ONE DAY, BOB SEES A PIMPLE, WHICH HE FEELS MAKES HIM LOOK LIKE A PIZZA...

©2009 F. DERUVO

WHAT BOB SEES...

WHAT WE SEE...

When you come right down to it, it is nothing less than being myopic. People tend to focus on one thing, which can often become all consuming, and with respect to the PreTrib Rapture position, it *is* all consuming.

Somewhere, in the not too distant past, someone was likely reading his Bible and came across the warnings of Paul and Peter describing what attitudes will be like in the End Times, prior to the Tribulation. This particular individual (probably not the brightest bulb in the carton), was so horrified about how lazy, spiteful, mean, rebellious, carnal, and unspiritual people would become, that he felt it necessary to classify the PreTrib Rapture as one of those things that causes this to occur, or is at least swept up in the ensuing deception.

Paul and Peter Warn Us

Let's look at the Scripture to which we are referring. In one of his letters to Timothy, Paul states, *"But understand this, that in the last days difficult times will come. For people will be lovers of themselves, lovers of money, boastful, arrogant, blasphemers, disobedient to parents, ungrateful, unholy, unloving, irreconcilable, slanderers, without self-control, savage, opposed to what is good, treacherous, reckless, conceited, loving pleasure rather than loving God. They will maintain the outward appearance of religion but will have repudiated its power. So avoid people like these. For some of these insinuate themselves into households and captivate weak women who are overwhelmed with sins and led along by various passions. Such women are always seeking instruction, yet never able to arrive at a knowledge of the truth. And just as Jannes and Jambres opposed Moses, so these people – who have warped minds and are disqualified in the faith – also oppose the truth. But they will not go much further, for their foolishness will be obvious to everyone, just like it was with Jannes and Jambres,"* (2 Timothy 3:1-9 NET).

Peter also comments on the tone of the times during the Last Days, *"But false prophets arose among the people, just as there will be false teachers among you. These false teachers will infiltrate your midst with destructive heresies, even to the point of denying the Master who bought them. As a result, they will bring swift destruction on themselves. And many will follow their debauched lifestyles. Because of these false teachers, the way of truth will be slandered. And in their greed they will exploit you with deceptive words. Their condemnation pronounced long* ago is not sitting idly by; their destruction is not asleep," (2 Peter 2:1-3 NET).

Mini-Olivet Here with Noah and Lot

Peter then highlights how God saved both Noah and Lot from the wrath of the God-directed global flood and the fire and brimstone that rained down from heaven, respectively; He knows how to save the righteous from fiery trials. Following this, he states, *"Brazen and insolent, they are not afraid to insult the glorious ones, yet even angels, who are much more powerful, do not bring a slanderous judgment against them before the Lord. But these men, like irrational animals – creatures of instinct, born to be caught and destroyed – do not understand whom they are insulting, and consequently in their destruction they will be destroyed, suffering harm as the wages for their harmful ways. By considering it a pleasure to carouse in broad daylight, they are stains and blemishes, indulging in their deceitful pleasures when they feast together with you. Their eyes, full of adultery, never stop sinning; they entice unstable people. They have trained their hearts for greed, these cursed children! By forsaking the right path they have gone astray, because they followed the way of Balaam son of Bosor, who loved the wages of unright-eousness, yet was rebuked for his own transgression (a dumb donkey, speaking with a human voice, restrained the prophet's madness).*

These men are waterless springs and mists driven by a storm, for whom the utter depths of darkness have been reserved. For by speaking high-sounding but empty words they are able to entice, with fleshly desires and with debauchery, people who have just escaped from those who reside in error. Although these false teachers promise such people freedom, they themselves are enslaved to immorality. For whatever a person succumbs to, to that he is enslaved. For if after they have escaped the filthy things of the world through the rich knowledge of our Lord and Savior Jesus Christ, they again get entangled in them and succumb to them, their last state has become worse for them than their first. For it would have been better for them never to have known the way of righteousness than, having known it, to turn back from the holy commandment that had been delivered to them. They are illustrations of this true proverb: 'A dog returns to its own vomit'" and 'A sow, after washing herself, wallows in the mire'," (2 Peter 2:10b-22 NET).

Between Paul and Peter, we have a fairly in-depth understanding of what the Last Days will be like to live in. Jesus highlights some of these very same things as well, in the Olivet Discourse, found in Matthew 24, Mark 13 and Luke 21. The point of all this is that men will become worse and worse as time moves toward the period we refer to as the Tribulation. Peter mentions "false prophets" and Paul describes them. It is clear from both that there will be people living during these times who are nothing more than spiritual charlatans, doing what they can to gain whatever they want. They will use people, present their teachings as truth, and will ultimately pull people away from the truth that is found in Christ.

Changing Salvation to Another Gospel
The main commonality between the false prophets that both Paul and Peter refer to is that they wind up drawing people *away* from the authentic gospel, to something that only outwardly *appears* to be the gospel, but in reality, is not. This is simply the way *all* false prophets work. Their ultimate end goal is to "fill their stomachs," or to take care of their own needs by building up their bank accounts.

Now into this huge can of apostasy are tossed all types of doctrines, sometimes by well-meaning people, who diligently seek to serve the Lord, and other times, but people who are not well meaning at all. Their objective is to further their cause, which usually has something to do with either making themselves or their doctrine pre-eminent.

Unfortunately, many of the doctrines that are routinely lumped together with others are not heresy at all, even though the doctrines *themselves* could be *incorrect*. For instance, when the thief on the cross was saved, after humbling himself, repenting of his unbelief and then meekly requesting that he be merely remembered when Jesus ruled over His coming kingdom, Jesus did not stop to ask him his views on Eschatology (the study of the Last Days). In fact, though some find it difficult to appreciate, the spiritual transaction that took place between Jesus and the thief that day, as they both hung dying, was very simple. It was not at all complicated in any way, which is the way Christianity is – *uncomplicated*.

The Simplicity of the Gospel

Christianity is deliberately *not* complex so that all can have the same opportunity to receive salvation. This is why Paul says preaching about Christ's death is foolishness to those who think themselves wise (cf. 1 Corinthians 1:18). Many are offended by the Gospel because it is *so* straightforward that it takes a child's simplicity to receive it. What *keeps* people from receiving salvation is an unwillingness to repent (to change one's mind), in humility about whom Jesus Christ is, and believe on Him.

Anything or anyone who attempts to pre-empt this spiritual transaction is clearly standing in opposition to the authentic gospel. If someone is attempting to draw someone else away from the gospel, by presenting them with some type of alternative, cleverly disguised in some cases, they are nothing more than false prophets because they present lies as truth.

Is the PreTrib Rapture Position Drawing People Away?

The PreTrib Rapture position is often seen as something that pulls people away from Christ, and since it is seen this way, then it is considered to be just as dangerous as anything a false prophet would preach. Nevertheless, the question must be asked, does the PreTrib Rapture position actually teach *another* gospel? If so, then it should be classified as heresy. If not, then it is without doubt *not* heresy.

In Steve Wohlberg's book, *End Times Delusions*, the author opens chapter one with these words that define the PreTrib Rapture, "*First, Jesus comes* invisibly *to remove His Church before a seven-year tribulation during which the rest of humanity must face the antichrist. This is the rapture. At the end of those seven years, Jesus will again return* visibly *to deliver those who became Christians during the tribulation – after being given a 'second chance' to be saved – and to pulverize the invading enemies of Israel at Armageddon.*"[1]

Hidden Seventh Day Adventist Teachings

Wohlberg is a Seventh Day Adventist, a group that originally began with the teachings and leadership of William Miller (they became known as Millerites). Because of a false understanding of Christ's Second Advent, a general date was given in which it was believed that Jesus would physically return to earth sometime between March of 1843 and March of 1844. When these dates came and went with no sign of His return, many followers became disillusioned and the event itself became known as The Great Disappointment.

A number of groups came out of this disillusionment and confusion, and the Great Disappointment was eventually seen not as Christ's physical return to earth, but an event during that time (between 1843 and 1844), which took place in heaven. From this, the more detailed belief summed up as the "Investigative Judgment," was believed to have convened in 1844 and continues to the present. It is explained as God's divine judgment on professed Christians.

Eventually, Ellen G. White, who was believed to have been a modern day prophet, furthered this view, and clarified numerous other positions held today within Seventh Day Adventism. Because of the controversy surrounding the beginnings of this group, as well as the biblical faux pas made throughout their history, especially with respect to the Second

---

[1] Steve Wohlberg, *End Times Delusion* (Treasure House 2005), 21

Advent of Christ, and salvation itself, one can only wonder how or why Seventh Day Adventists believe that their theology is the correct view and all others are incorrect.

Adventist Salvation

The failed prophecy of William Miller should be enough to set off red flag for people. Yet Seventh Day Adventism has maintained in spite of this blatant and exposed false teaching.

Part of the largest problem with Seventh Day Adventism is their view that ultimately, salvation is works-related. John R. Rice commenting on Seventh Day Adventism states, *"In article 9 (of 'What Seventh-Day Adventists Believe'), it says, 'that those who are truly converted and love God will diligently study, and give heed to, His Word.' And they give eight Scripture references and none of them say anything like that. The simple truth is that people who are converted do not always 'diligently study' the Bible and do not always obey it in many matters. This is a part of the doctrine of salvation by works which they teach, and that one may keep saved by keeping on working."*[2]

It is unfortunately clear that from the teachings of Ellen G. White, a view of salvation is taught, which I do not find in Scripture. This is the belief that up until the very end of a Christian's life, that individual cannot be sure of having received salvation. Without getting into a debate about eternal security and whether or not the Christian actually has it once becoming saved, I am in absolute disagreement over this teaching that a Christian can lose salvation. While some might argue that this view is nothing more than easy-believism, allowing Christians to live as they want to live without thought of repercussions related to sinful behavior, that in and of itself does not negate a doctrine that is taught in Scripture.

---

[2] John R. Rice *False Doctrines* (Sword of the Lord Publishers 1970), 183

In other words, if people find a way to abuse the doctrine of grace leading to salvation, that is not the fault of the Lord's. Moreover, it also does *not* mean that *if* a supposed loophole in the doctrine has been located, the doctrine cannot be true. This is a purely fabricated argument, which – as I have stated – I do not find in Scripture. The worth of a doctrine needs to be made based on the teaching of Scripture. For those who are interested in learning more about the subject of eternal security, there are many excellent books on the subject.

A Cult?

Ultimately, any group that has so many difficulties at its root, and has based at least some of its teachings on those, which turned out to be false, is a group that is likely best to avoid at all costs. At least in some respects, Seventh Day Adventism has characteristics of a cult.

To further the problem, Wohlberg seems unwilling to talk about the fact that he is a Seventh Day Adventist. The information is not provided in his book *End Time Delusions* that I could find. Beyond this, one has to search a great deal for it on his website. When asked about why he did not list this information, Wohlberg's response was *"I don't mention my personal denominational affiliation on my web site simply because the Word of God is much bigger than any church. Bible truth will endure forever, not the Seventh-day Adventist Church. My desire is to reach out to as many people as possible with the pure truth of God's Word. I am a follower of Jesus Christ first and a Seventh-day Adventist second. Jesus didn't say, "Go ye into all the world and tell everyone right away what church you belong to." He said, "Go ye into all the world and preach the gospel." Anytime anyone asks me, I gladly tell them my church affiliation without any shame. I often receive inquiries about this from readers of my books. I always tell them. Billy Graham is a Baptist, but he also has his "Billy Graham Evangelistic Association." There are thousands of non-*

Adventist ministries out there who also have web sites like mine that don't list denominational affiliation either."[3]

However, that is a bit of a copout. While of course God's Word is much larger than any church, people want to know (and have every right to know), what people believe. That is often best indicated (not always), by knowing to which religion and/or denomination a person is connected. Certainly, when cultists come to our door, espousing their beliefs in Christian-sounding terminology, it is very helpful to understand what they actually believe based on their denomination.

He Relents

Ultimately, Wohlberg did finally choose to list something, because on the "About Us" page of his website, the last sentence currently reads (as of the date of this writing; 12/28/2009), *"The Wohlbergs are members of the Newport Washington Seventh-day Adventist Church."*[4]

It is interesting what one is able to find when searching through the Internet. There are a number of websites advocating Wohlberg's books because of their alleged insight, truth and wisdom. A number of these websites boast beliefs, which are interestingly enough like Seventh Day Adventist beliefs, without stating it. One such site had a multitude of links posted, many of which were directly connected to other Seventh Day Adventist sites. Yet, the words "Seventh Day Adventist" do not appear on these sites (except possibly in the links they promote).

On another site, not necessarily connected with Wohlberg's, their "About Us" page reads in part, *"We are a self funded ministry dedicated to spreading the truth of God's Word. We believe and teach the same things that were taught by Jesus, as well as what Paul and the Apostles taught to the early Church."*[5] All well and good, except for the "self

---

[3] http://www.atomorrow.com/discus/messages/10021/5201.html?1108090644
[4] http://whitehorsemedia.com/about/
[5] http://www.wiccawitchcraft.net/about.html

funded ministry" part. Who are these people? What (if any) organization stands behind them? Why do they seem so unwilling to say who they are and what they represent? As one continues to peruse both their About Us page, their emphasis on believing and living the Ten Commandments and works comes to the fore.

Nope, Not Going to Say It and You Can't Make Me!
Toward the bottom of the page, the following statements were posted: *"It was never God's intention for His Church to be divided into multiple denominations and sadly, we have found through experience that many choose to judge what they read based on one's denomination. We also discovered that the more truth a Church has, the more lies the enemy has coming against it to keep people from finding truth. See who is the remnant Church for more information. After our first few thousand hours of study, it rapidly became more and more apparent that what is truth is not always popular and what is popular is not always truth. Mark Twain once said, 'A lie can travel halfway around the world, while truth puts on its shoes'."* and...

"Since having a denominational name gives Satan something to attack and many Christians have the tendency to judge truth by denomination rather than the Word of God, we have chosen not to reveal denomination. This decision was made with much prayer and ultimately so this ministry could be more effective in spreading truth to the world. The following scriptures inform us of what truth is and how it should be established and it is not by one's denomination. John 14:6 'Jesus saith unto him, I am the way and the TRUTH...' John 17:17 'Sanctify them through your Truth: your WORD is TRUTH.' 1 Thessalonians 2:13 '...when you received the Word of God which you heard of us, you received it not as the word of men, but as it is in TRUTH, the Word of God, which effectually worketh also in you that believe'."[6]

---

[6] http://www.wiccawitchcraft.net/about.html

However, their statements could easily be seen as simply a ruse, designed to keep readers from knowing who they are and what they teach.

Also note that they have set themselves up as:

- *Having a great deal of truth, possibly even more than others*
- *Their decision to not reveal their denominational identity came about through "much prayer"*

The Lord Spoke to Me (through Prayer)

Doesn't everyone say that *prayer* is the reason they do something? Of course they do. When it is solemnly stated that a decision was only arrived at after a good deal of prayer, then how can that be refuted (except through the Bible)? How can anyone respond with "Well, you obviously did not hear correctly, did you?"

On one hand, these folks say that God never intended there to be so many different denominations. It is sad, they say. They also note that listing a denominational name gives Satan more room to attack. On the other hand, they refuse to reveal the name of their denomination. The name of their denomination is obviously important to them; otherwise, why would they be part of that particular denomination? Would they not simply be "Christians at Large," or something similar, if name was not important? It is *because* they are part of a specific denomination, yet they have chosen to withhold the name of that denomination that their motives become suspect.

Would God actually lead someone to become part of a denomination that ultimately winds up being a secret organization (you cannot tell people the name of it because of all the dirt that is out there on it)? This is what we are effectively being told. Yes, these individuals *are* part of a denomination, but no, they are *not* going to reveal it to us. They do not have to reveal it, because by merely looking at their "About Us" page, it provides the information we need to know. It is nothing more than a child's game of subterfuge that they simply do not win.

Seventh Day Reputation Precedes Them

Could it be that Seventh Day Adventism, for most people, represents problematic theology? This would certainly explain why Wohlberg (and other Adventists), wishes not to be pigeonholed by people who know a good deal about Adventism. If so, then this is an overtly subtle, yet deceptive approach. They want to deceive the world into thinking that though they are Seventh Day Adventists, we should not believe all that "hogwash" that has apparently been written against their "denomination."

This is no different from when a Mormon or Jehovah's Witness comes to your door. They approach you with Christian-sounding terminology, but their meaning is normally quite different from orthodox Christianity. The last thing they are going to do is announce to you from across the street that they are members of cults who are there to proselytize you! Fortunately, it is become quite easy to know when a person from such a cult is approaching your door. Rather than be taken by surprise, it allows us the opportunity to pray, then speak to them, hopefully guiding them to the understanding that Jesus Christ is who He said He is and has done for humanity what He came to accomplish.

One other thing that is worthy to note. On the website about Wicca, there is a link to another site dealing with the Mark of the Beast. From there, a link is posted that reveals that there are **125 websites** associated with one particular company, and of which the Wicca and Mark of the Beast websites are included. Every one of the websites we checked out included the same information on the "About Us" page that we highlighted. It would appear that every one of these pages deals with "closet" Seventh Day Adventism. Who is deceiving whom? That is a large amount of websites, which is not cheap to create, host or manage. All the websites we checked were owned by the same individual as well.

Does Being Wrong Mean Being Deceived?
A comment needs to be made about Wohlberg's reference to people being given a "second chance," but first another quote. After Wohlberg points to The Left Behind series of books and movies, he asks, "*Although 'rapture' isn't a biblical word, is the doctrine there? If not, could it be an* end times **delusion**? *Let's find out.*"[7] (emphasis added)

Why does Wohlberg automatically conclude that if the PreTrib Rapture is not the correct Rapture position to hold, it could very well be based on *deception*? A number of people do this when referencing the PreTrib Rapture position, yet they seem to bypass the other Rapture positions with which they do not agree. Those other positions are merely *wrong*, yet not based on deception. This is reserved for the PreTrib Rapture position only, it would seem. Do we also have to mention (again), that though the word "rapture" is not in Scripture, the Greek word *harpazo* is which means to be "caught up"? Rapture has a similar meaning.

According to Wohlberg's stated beliefs on his website, of which he is listed as Director of his ministry, he believes that we are now living in the End Times. He further believes that "*The Antichrist of prophecy is already in the world.*"[8] Further, he believes that "*The major Protestant Reformers were correct about the Antichrist,*"[9] and that "*Jesus will not return secretly, but openly and visibly for all to see.*"[10]

According to one of the books written by Wohlberg, he also believes that the Mark of the Beast spoken about in the book of Revelation is none other than worshiping on Sunday, instead of Saturday. It is an

---

[7] Steve Wohlberg, *End Times Delusion* (Treasure House 2005), 22
[8] http://www.whitehorsemedia.com/about/beliefs.cfm
[9] http://www.whitehorsemedia.com/about/beliefs.cfm
[10] Ibid

interesting and convoluted trail that brings him to this point, but he goes through the Roman Catholic Church, and the pope to get to it. Since there is a good deal of symbolism in Revelation, then Steve wonders if the Mark of the Beast is also to be taken figuratively. He believes so, and begins by decoding the word "beast." Since each of the first four beasts in Daniel represented kingdoms, then the fifth beast also represents a kingdom. This kingdom – Rome – is equated with Romanism, or the Roman Catholic Church, and Wohlberg then equates the 11th Horn with that of the pope, head of the Roman Catholic Church.

Wohlberg then lists six characteristics of the Roman Catholic Church, which he believes match up with the identity of this beast, and therefore the mark. Since this "beast" (Roman Catholic Church, headed by the pope), has the power to change the times and laws (cf. Daniel 7:25), then it is simply a matter of moving one further step to show that the pope is indeed the beast and the mark is changing worship from Saturday to Sunday.[11]

Love and Respect?

It should also be noted that this very same statement of beliefs includes the mantra, *"We should treat everyone with love and respect."*[12] That is certainly fine, however, like many anti-PreTribbers, the love falls short when their attention is directed at those who believe and espouse the PreTrib Rapture position.

While this author certainly agrees with just about everything else listed in Wohlberg's statement of beliefs, it is difficult to understand how he marries the idea that "no one will know the day nor the hour" with the idea that "every eye will see Him." If the Tribulation is a period of seven years in length, then people will obviously be able to discern when Jesus will return.

---

[11] http://www.the-mark-of-the-beast.com/
[12] Ibid

However, Wohlberg does not believe that there is any time left in the 70 weeks of Daniel (chapter 9). He believes it has all been fulfilled and because he does, then what is left is that Christ will simply return at some unknown point in the future. No one knows when and there will not necessarily be any signs immediately preceding it. Therefore, for Wohlberg, there is no future Tribulation.

Second Chance?

Regarding Wohlberg's comment about people being given a second chance, it might be a good time to remind everyone that as long as people remain *alive*, they always have a chance to repent (change their mind about Jesus, His veracity, His trustworthiness, and His redemptive work on our behalf). This repentance will hopefully, lead to salvation, but it does not always do so.

There are people alive now, as you read this book, which have been given numerous chances by God to receive His salvation. For one reason or another, they refused, either by putting it off until another day, or by rejecting that truth outright, in favor of something else that they felt more comfortable believing.

Next week, these same people might be given another opportunity to receive Jesus. What they do then might be different from what they did now, or yesterday. It is only after a person *dies* that all chances to repent about Christ, and receive His salvation are gone...for all eternity.

The idea that the Rapture occurring before the Tribulation (snatching millions of people off this planet instantly), cannot be true because that would mean those "left behind" would be given an additional chance to receive salvation is patently absurd! Where did anyone get this idea that people who are *alive – living on this planet* come to the end of their opportunities to receive Christ? I do not find that in the Bible, do you?

There is nothing that teaches that God stops providing opportunities for salvation to people who are alive, but who have continuously rejected Him. God will give as many chances as necessary before they leave this earth.

If the Rapture does occur, and the people left behind do question it, and then some of those individuals realize the truth that it presents, and become Christians because of it, how is that biblically incorrect? I do not see it. Proof of that is the fact that not all those left behind *will* become Christians. Many will *continue* to reject Christ and His salvation.

This is no different from when Christ lived on this planet and on a daily basis, displayed His deity. During these times when He raised that person from the dead, healed that lame or infirm individual, fed the 5,000, or gave sight back to a blind man, He did these things because He was, and remains God. These miracles attested to that fact and verified the authenticity as Messiah.

Not Everyone Receives the Gospel at Their First Hearing
However, it is just as clear that in spite of the fact that though many people benefited from Christ's miracles, the Pharisees did not, nor did everyone who heard Him preach or witness His miracles become Christians. Each new day that Christ performed some new miracle, preached some new message, or did something else, which called attention to the fact that He was Messiah; a new opportunity presented itself to these religious leaders to change their mind about Christ. In essence then, each new day or situation provided a "second chance" for these individuals.

These people lived among Christ and His disciples. They saw His continued acts of compassion and kindness and they heard His words, which cut them to the quick. Time after time, they were given second chance after second chance to receive His Truth about Him according to the Scriptures. They often refused, though some did turn to Him. All of them could have changed their mind about Christ at any moment. Nicodemus did, in what is likely the most famous passage regarding salvation, found in John 3.

The thief on the cross eventually changed his mind about Jesus and we have absolutely no idea how many times he may have heard Christ preach (or not), and saw His miracles (or not). The New Testament is filled with examples of the numerous chances that one individual after another had to change their minds. Why? Because God is, above all, compassionate and loving.

Yes, His wrath, stemming from His holiness, will be poured out on the earth during the seven-year period known as the Tribulation, however, even in that period, people will come to know Him as Savior. There will be too many who do not, even after they witness miracle after miracle.

The two witnesses in Revelation are there to evangelize all of humanity. It is clear that the whole world hates them and wants them dead. The Antichrist gives them their wish and the world celebrates for three days! Finally, God raises them up and then calls them up to heaven. This of course, freaks out the citizens of this world, but not enough to change their opinion of Christ.

The belief that God, by providing second chances for people to receive Him as Savior and Lord after witnessing some huge miracle, is biblically incorrect is patently wrong. This is merely another argument against the PreTrib Rapture position that is fully manufactured. It is a straw man argument having no basis in biblical fact. People *saw* the Messiah. They touched Him. They ate food He created from a few fish and loaves. The people of His day heard Him speak on many occasions. Not all of these people initially turned to Him in faith. Many never turned to Him in faith. Yet, God kept providing additional chances for them to come to Him.

Chance After Chance After Chance...*If* Necessary

Every day, people receive a second, a third, a fourth, or a tenth chance to receive Christ, by repenting (changing their opinion about who Christ is), which hopefully leads to salvation. Yet, everyday, many of these same people will continue to reject Christ. Is it all right with you (or Steve Wohlberg), if God chooses to give them yet another chance to receive His salvation? Fortunately, He is not asking us. He is doing what He has chosen to do and whether we like it or not, that is what He does.

How many times did it take *you* to hear about Jesus before you repented unto salvation? How many times was it; once, twice, three times, or more? Was it twenty-five times or more? Aren't you glad that God persevered? I know that I am where I am concerned.

However, Wohlberg has just started. He now, seemingly with tongue firmly planted in cheek, continues to dissect for us Paul's passage in 1 Thessalonians 4:16-17 for us. This passage is one of the main passages, which deals with the Rapture. The passage in question states, *"For the Lord himself shall descend from heaven with a shout, with the voice of the archangel, and with the trump of God: and the dead in Christ shall rise first: Then we which are alive and remain shall be caught up together with them in the clouds, to meet the Lord in the air: and so shall we ever be with the Lord."*

If a Trumpet Sounds in the Forest Does Anyone Hear It?

Wohlberg comments on this by stating, *"Rapture teachers interpret this event as silent and secret, yet doesn't it seem rather loud and visible? There is a shout, a voice, a trumpet. Have you ever heard of a silent trumpet? The truth is, 1 Thessalonians 4:16 is one of the noisiest verses in the Bible! Look carefully: Jesus Christ comes down from heaven shouting and blowing a trumpet. The dead rise. Then true believers are 'caught up.' Honestly, do you see anything here about vanishing Christians prior to the tribulation? Rapture promoters interpret 'caught up' to mean* disappear *because this view fits their rightly-meshed prophetic system, yet it must be admitted that the text doesn't say this."*[13]

I am going to try to be nice here, in spite of the fact that Wohlberg has left himself wide open for rebuke and criticism. Turn to the book of Acts, chapter 8. What do you see when you start reading at verse twenty-five? You read about the Ethiopian eunuch. The passage says, *"So, when they had solemnly testified and spoken the word of the Lord, they started back to Jerusalem, and were preaching the gospel to many villages of the Samaritans. But an angel of the Lord spoke to Philip saying, "Get up and go south to the road that descends from Jerusalem to Gaza." (This is a desert road.) So he got up and went; and there was an Ethiopian eunuch, a court official of Candace, queen of the Ethiopians, who was in charge of all her treasure; and he had come to Jerusalem to worship, and he was returning and sitting in his chariot, and was reading the prophet Isaiah. Then the Spirit said to Philip, "Go up and join this chariot,"* (Acts 8:25-29 NASB).

In this section, we see a number of supernatural events occurring:

- *An angel of the Lord speaks to Philip, giving him an assignment*
- *The Holy Spirit speaks to Philip, telling him to join the eunuch on his chariot*

Exactly Who Heard the Holy Spirit?
Does the text say whether either of these messages to Philip was spoken *aloud*? Can we dogmatically say that either the angel or the Holy Spirit spoke aloud to Philip? We really cannot say with certainty. The most we can do is say that either the angel or Holy Spirit spoke aloud to Philip or they spoke through his thoughts, or the angel spoke aloud and the Holy Spirit spoke through Philip's thoughts (or vice versa). That is the

---

[13] Steve Wohlberg, *End Times Delusion* (Treasure House 2005), 22-23

most we can do. We may be able to dig into the original languages to determine whether the word "spoke," related to the angel is a word that means spoken aloud, but even that may not provide us with a final word on the subject.

What we know is that the angel and the Holy Spirit communicated with Philip in some manner so that their intentions were clearly known to Philip. Because their intentions were clearly understood by Philip, he had no difficulty obeying.

Were there others around Philip at the time the angel and the Holy Spirit spoke to Philip? If so, what, if anything did they actually hear?

The Supernatural is Always Heard or Seen
Like many of his interpretations, I believe Wohlberg is on slippery ground here with his understanding of the text because he is guilty of interpreting a completely supernatural event, in a completely *non-supernatural* way. Wohlberg assumes that when God blows a trumpet, everyone will hear it (and by the way, the text does not say that Jesus Himself will blow the trumpet. It merely says He descends with a shout and the trump of God). He assumes that supernatural events are events that *must follow* the natural laws of physics and other scientific laws within our own sphere of reality. Is this the case though?

What occurred once Philip had completed his assignment with the Ethiopian eunuch? The text reads, "*When they came up out of the water, the Spirit of the Lord snatched Philip away; and the eunuch no longer saw him, but went on his way rejoicing. But Philip found himself at Azotus, and as he passed through he kept preaching the gospel to all the cities until he came to Caesarea,*" (Acts 8:39-40 NASB).

We read that just as they came up out of the water (Philip has just baptized the Ethiopian eunuch in water), the Spirit of the Lord literally whisked Philip away! One second he was there, and the next second he was completely gone from view. Notice the last verse states that Philip "found himself at Azotus." Apparently, the Holy Spirit took Philip away, instantly placing him somewhere else geographically. Was there any noise associated with this movement by the Holy Spirit? Who knows? Do we know what it looked like to the Ethiopian, or what it felt like to Philip? We have no idea at all.

Let us consider another example. In the next chapter of Acts, Saul is converted. He is on his way to Damascus to capture and bring back Jews who have begun following Jesus Christ, forsaking Judaism. This is not good for the nation of Israel, to allow these heretics to continue. They must be rounded up and punished, put to death if they do not retract their conversion.

Did You Hear and See That?
On the way, Saul is overcome by a tremendous light and he hears a voice, the voice of Jesus asking him why he was persecuting him. Because of this event, Saul repents (changes his mind about Jesus Christ), which led to salvation. This light was obviously brighter than the sun, since the text states that this happened at midday.

Notice the text states that "*The men who traveled with him stood speechless, hearing the voice but seeing no one,*" (Acts 9:7 NASB). So these men heard a voice, but they saw nothing. We do not even know from this sentence whether they actually heard *words*. It simply says they heard a voice. Go to a busy restaurant some time. You will hear plenty of voices, but it is likely that you will not be able to make out what is being said. It is just the noise of voices.

If we follow Wohlberg's logic, we would have to say that they heard the exact same thing that Saul heard, because though this was a supernatural event, if Paul heard it, everyone must have heard it. Later on in the same book of Acts, Paul recounts this story as defense for himself before other Jews who were attempting to try him on charges.

Paul states during his defense, *"And those who were with me saw the light, to be sure, but did not understand the voice of the One who was speaking to me,"* (Acts 22:9 NASB). Ah, so it becomes clear then that the men, who were with Paul on that road to Damascus, did actually see the light, and while they heard the voice, they had no clue what was being said.

How could this be though? They were with Paul, weren't they? If they were with Paul and only a few feet from him, and they heard a voice, how could they *not* have heard exactly what Paul heard? The answer is simply because this was clearly a supernatural event, and because it was supernatural, it did not follow the normal rules that all things must follow in our physical realm. What Jesus said to Paul were for Paul's ears *only*.

Wouldn't Falling Chains Make Noise?

One more example should hopefully, suffice. Turn to Acts 12. Here we read of Peter's imprisonment and eventual escape. How did he escape? Let's read the text. *"And behold, an angel of the Lord suddenly appeared and a light shone in the cell; and he struck Peter's side and woke him up, saying, "Get up quickly" And his chains fell off his hands. And the angel said to him, "Gird yourself and put on your sandals." And he did so. And he said to him, "Wrap your cloak around you and follow me." And he went out and continued to follow, and he did not know that what was being done by the angel was real, but thought he was seeing a vision. When they had passed the first and second guard, they came to the iron gate that leads into the city, which opened for them by itself; and they went out and went along one street, and immediately the angel departed from him,"* (Acts 12:7-10 NASB).

Is Peter Houdini?

Here is Peter, solidly locked in jail, being guarded by two guards, one on each side of him. Normally, there would have been one on each side, to keep him securely in chains, and Peter would have been chained to each guard. What is the sequence of events here though?

- *An angel of the Lord appears*
- *A light shined in the cell*
- *The angel strikes Peter's side*
- *The angel speaks to Peter*
- *The chains simply fall away*
- *The angel leads the way past the first and second guards*
- *They arrive at the city gate and it opens by itself*
- *The traveled a ways down a street and then – poof! – the angel is gone*

The above sequence of events is interesting. As the angel appears, a light shines in the cell. Except for a lit torch here and there, the cell would have been dark. Funny thing is that neither guard seems to have noticed this intensely bright light. Interesting. The angel then strikes Peter's side to wake him (and proves that this angel has substance).

Quiet on the Set!
The heavy chains that bound Peter simply fall away. Unless they were made of feathers, they would have made considerable noise, even being moved around, much less hitting the ground. Funny thing is that neither guard notices the noise of the chains falling either. Had they died and simply not fallen over yet? Wonder what happened?

The angel then leads Peter past the first guard and the second guard. Again, neither guard notices. Hmmm, this is just way too suspicious! I know! The angel must have drugged the guards! That's it! Why else would they completely miss everything that is happening?

Finally, the angel and Peter arrive at the heavy iron gate and it supernaturally opens by itself. After leading Peter down a street, he vanishes without a trace. Of course, this entire time, Peter thought he was having a dream or a vision. It was only after the angel vanished that Peter realized that it had not been a dream.

What is the point to all of these examples? Simply put, these are supernatural events. It is clear that in many cases, the only people who hear, see and/or experience things of a supernatural nature are those of *God's own choosing*.

Just as Stephen was being stoned to death, he looked up in the sky and saw Jesus Christ standing. Stephen took the time to point that out to the crowd. Did they see it? Probably not. Had they seen it, they likely would have dropped their stones.

Steve Wohlberg believes that the 1 Thessalonians 4:16-17 passage cannot be referring to any type of Rapture. Why? Because the event itself is just too darn noisy. I mean, how could God shout, blow a trumpet and call up the dead, then call those who are alive, without the entire world hearing it? Gee, I don't know, but I'm guessing that it is only His *sheep* who actually know His voice and can therefore hear Him. How He chooses to get the attention of His sheep is up to Him entirely.

Is it possible that this supernatural event described by Paul is *only for the Church* and if it is only for the Church, then is it possible that only those within the *authentic* Church will hear, see and experience it? As we have seen, not only is this possible, but *probable*, based on just these few examples I have culled from God's Word.

We must never assume that the supernatural has to obey the same laws as the natural. This is simply not the case at all. After Christ rose from the dead, He was able to walk through walls and doors without opening them, yet He could also be felt and it is implied that He ate!

Myopia means that we see things only one way because our focus is so narrow. Mr. Wohlberg accuses PreTrib Rapturists of two things:

1. *Being deceived*
2. *Forcing their beliefs onto Scripture, whether those beliefs fit or not*

The truth is though that Wohlberg himself is the one who is attempting to force the supernatural to act as if it is *natural*. He reads the text and thinks, "*Oh, there's a trumpet and a shout. Okay, so everyone would hear that. How could it be otherwise?*" Then he laughs, and gently shakes his head, thinking how stupid the PreTrib Rapturist is for not being able to discern the obvious. It *can* be otherwise and likely *is* otherwise for reasons already shown. Do you see how Wohlberg is superimposing his own beliefs and understanding on top of Scripture, to validate his own theology?

Wohlberg has no right to assume because *he* believes that the supernatural should act just like the natural, it is permissible for him to castigate those who do not see things as he does. How many times in Scripture has God revealed a vision, or a word to someone, yet those around that person do not hear or see the same thing? Apparently, either Wohlberg has forgotten all those times in Scripture, or he believes because the 1 Thessalonians 4:16-17 passage has to do with Christ's return, then His shout and the accompanying trumpet call would *naturally* be heard by everyone throughout the world. He does this because he believes that this passage is referencing Christ's Second Coming, which is visible and in which every eye will see Him. Could this passage possibly be referencing the Rapture?

The unfortunate part is that Wohlberg, while attempting to disprove the PreTrib Rapture position, does incredible injustice to the text of Scripture by interpreting it with his own template placed firmly over it. In essence, he is guilty of doing exactly what he accuses the PreTrib Rapturist of doing.

Chapter 2

Daniel's 70 Weeks

©2010 F. DERUVO

There is much debate and speculation over four specific verses in the book of Daniel, chapter 9. There are any number of proposed theories and suggestions about the meaning of these four verses. This is the only place in the entire Bible that this scenario of Daniel's 70 weeks appears. There is no other place in Scripture to ascertain the meaning of Daniel 9:24-27. There is nothing to compare it to. Therefore, the meaning must be gleaned from those verses and the context itself.

Could Steve Be Wrong?

Steve Wohlberg has written a number of articles on the Tribulation, as related to this Daniel 9:24-27 passage. Since he has arrived at conclusions that I believe to be in error, I thought it best to include some of his comments within the pages of this book and then point out where I believe he makes his errors.

His two-part article called "7 Years of Tribulation?" consists of attempting to determine the length of the 70 weeks that are outlined in this passage, and from there, he attempts to address whether or not the Tribulation has occurred or is still in the future.

Wohlberg also has another article titled "The 70th Week of Daniel Delusion" (he apparently likes that word "delusion," especially as it relates to those who believe and espouse the Rapture). In this article, he attempts to show that Scripture does not in any way, shape, or form, detail a period of 7 years for the Tribulation period. Let's start with this article and go on from there.

Shocking You Say?

Wohlberg begins his article by introducing the subject, and then says, *"Does the Bible really predict a future "seven-year period of tribulation" in the first place?"*[14] Predictably, he answers his own question with this comment, *"Shockingly, there is no specific Bible text predicting any seven-year tribulation."*[15] I would not mind if Wohlberg offered his *opinion* about this (which is what he is actually doing), but he makes that a declarative statement, in which it is quite clear that no one should deign to disagree with him.

Wohlberg refers to the Daniel 9:24-27 passage, and then refers to "modern" interpreters as those who have created the situation around

---

[14] http://www.whitehorsemedia.com/articles/details.cfm?art=33
[15] Ibid

which the Tribulation and its seven years are built. Therefore, preferring the interpreters of like mind from prior centuries, Wohlberg quotes Matthew Henry, Methodist Adam Clarke, and Jamieson, Fauccet, Brown.

That's a Wrap!
From here, Wohlberg states without equivocation, *"The following ten points provide solid evidence that Daniel's 70th week doesn't refer to any future Tribulation at all. Rather, it was fulfilled nearly two thousand years ago."*[16] This is often the position of Reformed, or Covenant Theologians, as well as Preterists. A plethora of books have been published about this issue, from a variety of theological perspectives. Take your pick of books and writers.

The actual text of Daniel states, *"Seventy weeks have been decreed for your people and your holy city, to finish the transgression, to make an end of sin, to make atonement for iniquity, to bring in everlasting righteousness, to seal up vision and prophecy and to anoint the most holy place. 'So you are to know and discern that from the issuing of a decree to restore and rebuild Jerusalem until Messiah the Prince there will be seven weeks and sixty-two weeks; it will be built again, with plaza and moat, even in times of distress. Then after the sixty-two weeks the Messiah will be cut off and have nothing, and the people of the prince who is to come will destroy the city and the sanctuary. And its end will come with a flood; even to the end there will be war; desolations are determined. And he will make a firm covenant with the many for one week, but in the middle of the week he will put a stop to sacrifice and grain offering; and on the wing of abominations will come one who makes desolate, even until a complete destruction, one that is decreed, is poured out on the one who makes desolate,"* (Daniel 9:24-27 NASB).

---

[16] http://www.whitehorsemedia.com/articles/details.cfm?art=33

Wohlberg's Ten Points

In paraphrasing Wohlberg's points from his previously mentioned article, they can be expressed as the following:

1. *Believes the entire 70 weeks should be taken to mean 70 weeks consecutively, with no break*
2. *Says there is absolutely no break between the 69th and 70th week, otherwise the 70th week should be called something else*
3. *Inserting a 2,000 year gap between weeks 69 and 70 is completely illogical*
4. *Wohlberg does not believe that Daniel 9:27 mentions:*
   a. *The Tribulation*
   b. *Rebuilt temple*
   c. *Antichrist*
5. *Believes the entire section – Daniel 9:24-27 – speaks of Messiah*
6. *States the word 'covenant' always refers to Messiah*
7. *Believes the phrase 'Confirming the covenant with many' means that Christ died for many*
8. *Says the middle of the week was when Christ died*
9. *Believes the 'overspreading of abomination' refers to what the religious leaders did to Jesus by crucifying Him*
10. *Says the 70 weeks applied to the Jewish people*

A correct view of Eschatology does not hinge upon a person's salvation. If it did, far fewer people would actually be saved. All I can say to that is, Thank the Lord for His graciousness!

Points 1 & 2 – All 70 Weeks Must Run Concurrently

Let me begin with number one and briefly go through all ten points. Points one and two are similar, so I will deal with them together. Wohlberg claims that for the 70th week to be the 70th week, it must fall immediately after the 69th week. If it does not, then it cannot be the 70th week.

By way of human example, Wohlberg provides the following: *"Note: If you told your child to be in bed in 70 minutes, you obviously would mean 70 consecutive minutes. What if five hours later your fully awake son said, "But dad, I know 69 minutes have passed, but the 70th minute hasn't started yet!"? After receiving an appropriate punishment, he would be swiftly sent to bed."*[17]

That is the best example with which he could come up? Forget that it is not even realistic, except possibly for a legalist. However, Steve, what if Dad set a timer and the timer unfortunately stopped at minute 69? Would the kid have a point then?

Wohlberg further claims that there is no place in any other portion of Scripture in which a time period stops then starts again. Additionally, he states that all biblical references to time periods are consecutive and I believe that we could also take that to mean that things in the Bible are chronological.

The problem though is that this is not entirely true. Even a cursory reading of Revelation shows things to be out of order (or as in the Olivet Discourse). Not everything is so neat and nice as Wohlberg would have us believe. If they were, he might have a solid argument, but since he is actually incorrect, his argument does not stand. I have dealt with Daniel 9:24-27 and the Olivet Discourse in other books I have written, so unfortunately, not a good deal of space will be taken up here to present these same articles. My rebuttal to Wohlberg's assertions[18] here is then to be considered abbreviated.

In the Olivet Discourse, there are things that are not chronological there. They are out of order. Besides this, the phrase "with the Lord, one day

---

[17] http://www.whitehorsemedia.com/articles/details.cfm?art=47
[18] Please look for the books *Between Weeks* and *The Anti-Supernatural Bias of Ex-Christians*, both by Fred DeRuvo and available at www.studygrowknow.com

is as a thousand years" (cf. 2 Peter 3:8), must be referenced here. There are a number of stated meanings to that one.

While Wohlberg is not necessarily guilty of allegorizing Scripture at this point, he still arrives at an errant position (in my opinion), due to what appears to be his misunderstanding of the meaning of the actual text.

It cannot reasonably be argued that because time is constantly moving forward, all of God's plans and purposes are on the *same* timeline. Yet, this is what Wohlberg expects us to believe; that things happen one after the other in perfect succession. Because of this, Wohlberg sees a problem when someone states there is some type or gap between areas of Scripture (represented in real time). This cannot be, he says.

Time Out!
However, please consider your own life and all that transpires in it during the course of a day. You get up, you prepare for work or school, you go to work or school and at the end of the day, you return home. Possibly, in the evening, you prepare for some other event as well. While you are doing your thing, other people are doing theirs. In fact, depending upon the time of year it is, any number of sporting events takes place during the same time frame in which you live, yet they are not on your time schedule at all.

Apparently, Wohlberg is not familiar with a variety of ways events are measured in time. Sporting events for instance, have their own clock. They go by their own schedule. Ever been to a professional basketball game, or watched the NBA on television? If you have, you know that when the game starts, the clock does not continuously count down the moments. In fact, every time someone is fouled, the ball goes out of bounds, or an official calls some type of infraction against one of the players, the game clock *stops*. However, the watch on your wrist does not stop, does it? Time continues to move on in real time. The timer for the game has stopped for a brief period of time. Between quarters, game time stops for a longer period.

There are so many things occurring in Scripture that it is difficult to keep track of them. We tend to view all the events of Scripture in a linear fashion, meaning that all of them line up end to end and simply occur at their appointed time, one after the other. This is not necessarily the case though. When prophecy was revealed to human beings from God or one of His angels, often, exact chronological time lines were not necessarily given.

Wohlberg categorically states, *"There is no example in Scripture (or anywhere else!) of a time period starting, stopping, and then starting again. All biblical references to time are consecutive: 40 days and 40 nights (Genesis 7:4), 400 years in Egypt (Genesis 15:13), etc."*[19] The problem though is that in areas where prophecy was uttered, time lines are not necessarily provided in specifics, nor does that prophetic utterance provide all the details. Wohlberg points to 40 days and 40 nights, but what does this actual time have to do with areas of prophecy? The two cannot necessarily be equated, connected or paralleled, yet Wohlberg seems not to differentiate between the often far-future look of prophecy, and the everyday occurrence of real time, in a linear fashion, such as God's Creation.

What about Joshua and the sun standing still (cf. Joshua 10)? Though the sun appeared to stop, (we all know the earth actually would have stopped revolving), time continued to march onward. In effect, there were two periods of time that day; one in which Joshua and the Israelites fought and one which measured how long the earth stood still.

A quick look in Revelation 8 also shows us that an *interlude* takes place in God's prophetic timetable. Where does this interlude occur?

---

[19] http://www.whitehorsemedia.com/articles/details.cfm?art=33

According to the text of Revelation 8, it occurs in heaven. The interlude lasted for roughly one half hour (cf. Revelation 8:1). Did that same interlude occur on the earth? Did everyone on earth stop what they were doing and then listened and waited? Not at all. In fact, when we see things occurring in heaven, the scene is often completely different from what we see occurring on earth. The time length (compared to earth), could also be different, since heaven is outside the bounds of time.

Consider Revelation 12. Everything is cruising along nicely in the book and then we arrive at chapter 12 and it seems out of place. It is not so weird once it is understood to be an overview of sorts, of redemption, beginning with the history of Israel from birth, to the arrival of Jesus at His first advent. Verses one through five start from the birth of Israel, to the birth of Christ, and Satan's attempts to destroy Him. From there, we see that this child (Christ), who came from the nation of Israel, is literally caught up into heaven and will ultimately rule the nations with a rod of iron. This speaks of Christ's death, resurrection and ascension.

Verse six picks up with Israel in the wilderness where she will be nourished for 1260 days. This verse speaks an event, which has not occurred yet.

Point 3 – A 2,000-year Gap is Illogical

Wohlberg's third point is similar to his first and second. He simply states that having a 2,000-year gap between week 69 and week 70 is illogical. He offers nothing more than saying it is illogical. If we go back to our basketball scenario, when the game time clock stops, the minutes in real time continue. Say the game clock stops at 4 minutes, 13 seconds. When the ball is put back into play, the clock does not take into account all the time that has gone by in real time. It merely starts from where it left off, at 4 minutes, 13 seconds.

Would Wohlberg also state that game clocks in sporting events are illogical, that there should be no time out, or that the game clock should never stop? I cannot imagine it, yet when it comes to God's "game" (we call the prophecy timeline), His clock is all of a sudden illogical?

But what of the charge that having a GAP between the second and third divisions of the 70 weeks is illogical? First, we are dealing with the supernatural, yet Wohlberg seems to insist on wanting to deal with the supernatural by dealing with it as if it is in the natural realm. Because a GAP seems illogical to him, that in and of itself cancels out any validity it might otherwise have, since God only deals in the logical. Really?

Logical or Illogical?

Let us take a closer look at this then. Is there anything else in the Bible that might appear to be *illogical*? We can probably come up with a few things without even breaking a sweat.

1. **The Trinity** – Three separate Persons in One. Illogical.
2. **Salvation** – God became Man, lived among us completely without sin, died a brutally horrific death; shed His blood for humanity, in order to pay our debt. Totally illogical. Makes no sense at all.
3. **Noah** - Are we really expected to believe that God sent all types of creatures to Noah? Are we to understand that Noah built a ship large enough to carry these animals, and any food they may have needed for the duration (roughly a year) of their time on top of the water? What about potable water? How is it possible that Noah could have stored enough drinking water for the trip, so that not one animal or person would die of thirst? Sounds extremely illogical.
4. **Abraham** – There are a number of things about God's dealings with Abraham that are completely illogical. Isaac of course, is the most illogical. Abraham, being roughly 100 years old, and his

wife Sarah nearly 80, she still manages to give birth! Absolutely illogical.

5. **Burning Bush** – How could a bush burn with fire and yet not be destroyed? Illogical.

6. **Balaam** – A donkey speaks?! (cf. Numbers 22) This is completely illogical. Animals do not speak Hebrew, or English or any other human tongue.

7. **Sun Stands Still** – No way! How could the earth actually stop rotating so that the sun appeared to stand still? (cf. Joshua 10) This must be a misprint. The earth does not stop rotating without creating massive problems...does it? Illogical.

8. **Giants** – Genesis 6 speaks of the fact that giants roamed the earth. Real giants? How could that be? Yet, we learn that Goliath was just over 9 feet tall and yet he was the smallest of his brothers! (cf. 1 Samuel 17) Another fable.

9. **Red Sea** - In Exodus, we learn that the Red Sea parted (as did the Jordan River in the book of Joshua). What? Come on and give me something I can believe, all right? It is completely illogical that water could split into two parts, with one side separating itself from the other side, allowing the Israelites to pass on dry ground. Illogical.

10. **Jesus** – Here are just a few situations related to Jesus.
    a. *Walking on Water*
    b. *Walking through Walls and Doors*
    c. *Recreating Eyes for a Blind Person*
    d. *Feeding 5,000*
    e. *Feeding 10,000*
    f. *Raising the Dead*

11. **Paul** – Paul is stoned and left for dead in the book of Acts. The disciples gather around him, he then miraculously gets up and heads back into the city. Hmmm, I don't know...sounds totally illogical to me.

These are merely a few examples from Scripture. It would be easy to continue, highlighting a book full of events and situations from the Bible, which clearly ask us to suspend our disbelief because they are completely illogical, from a human perspective. Yet, this is part of the nature of God. This is how He has chosen to work, where humanity is concerned. God, at times, appears completely illogical to us. One thing we often forget is that God is supernatural, and as such, He is completely beyond our natural realm. He is not affected by any laws that we are affected by.

If God decided to divide 70 weeks into three sections, and have the first two sections run concurrently, with a GAP of indeterminate length between the second and third GAP, what is that to us? Because it might seem "illogical" is not reason enough to discount it.

How Then to Interpret Prophecy?
In truth, the Bible is filled with one illogical event after another, which is why so many people have such a problem with much of it. In fact, theologians like Wohlberg have a great difficulty understanding prophecy in a literal (*not* litera*listic*, please), fashion. Because of his own Reformed background, he seems to have simply adopted the way the Reformers thought regarding Eschatology. I could easily argue that it is completely illogical to understand the Bible in literal terms, until arriving at prophetic areas of Scripture. These – it is said – must always be understood symbolically, or allegorically. There is nothing logical about the seemingly arbitrary decision to see God's Word that way, yet this is the modus operandi of many theologians today. When considering prophecy, it is immediately relegated to the opinions of the allegorist. Anyone who deigns to interpret prophetic discourse literally is shouted down or ridiculed.

This is what is happening here, with Wohlberg's interpretation of Daniel 9. He does not buy it and because of that, he has done his best to negate the possibility that there *is* a GAP between the 69th and 70th weeks. He has also created many straw man arguments that have no basis in faith or reality.

He appears to be working very hard to discount the possibility that he might be wrong. Look, as author of this book and others, I acknowledge that I could certainly be wrong about things, and I am more than happy to admit that possibility. In fact, it takes the pressure off me. I do not believe for one moment that I am correct about everything I believe; that all my theology is 100% right where it should be. I do not believe that when I stand before Jesus, He will say to me something like, *"Great job, Fred! You were 100% correct about every area of theology! You never made a mistake!"* It is absurd to think that will happen, that in this life, I will arrive at a point where I do not need to learn anything more, or that my theology is perfectly in tune with the Master.

To hear some authors talk, with their declarative statements, they are correct, and anyone who believes differently is 100% wrong. It would not hurt if more theologians used phrases like "In my opinion," or "I believe the text is stating." Instead, not only is every theologian an authority, but they wield words like "deceived," "deluded," "apostasy," and "heretic" like a club or sword. They seem to ready and willing to unsheathe their weapons at the drop of a hat, in order to beat everyone else over the head. Where is Vern Poythress when you need him?

Preterism

Not long ago, I spoke with a very well known Preterist, who has written a number of books, and also has his own radio program, etc., yada, yada, yada. During the course of our conversation, (of which the entirety was Eschatology), I finally asked him why his main concern had to do with Eschatology. For the number of listeners he had, he seemed only interested in proving non-Preterists wrong. Why was he not taking that time on the air to *evangelize* the lost? When I asked him, he had absolutely no answer for me, but instead, continued complaining about how wrong the Premillennialist is and how they should be silenced, etc. The question is how is he fulfilling Christ's mandate to evangelize the lost? Frankly, he does not appear to be, and what is worse is that this fact did not appear to bother him.

Dave MacPherson seems to have done the same thing. He has written eight books about one subject: the PreTrib Rapture. Why is he so concerned about this subject, when people are literally (not allegorically), leaving this life and arriving in hell, daily? This is completely *illogical* to me.

Though the byline on Wohlberg's website is *"Proclaiming His Salvation, Truth and Triumphant Return,"* there seems to be precious little on his the home page in which salvation is taught. In all fairness, I have no idea how often his home page is changed, but the number of times I visited during the month of December, as I wrote this book, the topics all dealt with either politics or End Times subjects. Why do people do this?

As Wohlberg implied at the beginning of one of his articles regarding the PreTrib Rapture, he believes it could very well be part of the End Times deception. Because he and others believe it to be part of the deception, they believe they must fight against it, because they believe that it somehow connects with salvation itself, or will keep people from it.

Point 4 & 5 – No Tribulation, Temple, or Antichrist Mentioned
I gave Wohlberg the benefit of the doubt with respect to what he thinks Daniel 9:24-27 does *not* include. He did not say that **he believes** these verses do not include references to the tribulation, the temple or the Antichrist. He stated without equivocation that they do not reference those things. However, he should have prefaced his remarks with his *belief*, because he cannot prove his own statement. Some will argue that I cannot prove mine either, but I am simply presenting an *opinion* of

what I believe the passage states. The reader should make up his or her own mind.

It is difficult not to view Wohlberg's opinion as a bit amateurish really, because though the passage does not use the words "tribulation," "temple," or "antichrist," arguments can be made to show that they are there. In verse 24, reference is made to a "holy place." While the Bible does not use the word "trinity," it can be shown that God is triune.

With respect to the phrase, a "holy place," people disagree about its meaning. Could it possibly reference the inner portion of the Temple? It could and there is no reason why it cannot. Verse 25 speaks of rebuilding Jerusalem. How could Jerusalem be said to be fully rebuilt if the Temple also is not reconstructed? This is the situation today in Israel, and as far as the Jews are concerned, Jerusalem is not finished, because the Temple has not been rebuilt. It is something they are moving rapidly toward and believe they will complete.

Verse 26 indicates, *"the people of the prince who is to come will destroy the city and the sanctuary."* Here, please note the mention of the word "sanctuary" which can also be taken to mean Temple, or a place of worship. Wohlberg is sure that *"This refers to the destruction of Jerusalem by Roman armies led by Prince Titus in A.D. 70."*[20] This is certainly one way of looking at it, but again, it is difficult to be dogmatic about it, yet Wohlberg is dogmatic about it. This is a classic Preterist, Reformed or Covenant position. Since this occurred in AD 70, the Tribulation has also already occurred.

While I actually *agree* with him that this is a reference to the destruction of Jerusalem and the Temple in A.D. 70, I *disagree* that this proves the Tribulation has already come and gone. I also disagree with him over the identity of the "prince who is to come."

---

[20] http://www.whitehorsemedia.com/articles/details.cfm?art=33

This event – the destruction of Jerusalem – to me is clearly in fulfillment of Jesus' words to his disciples that not one stone would stand upon another (cf. Matthew 24). Please note that Wohlberg states that there is no mention of the rebuilt Temple in this passage. However, it should be obvious to him that if he is going to state unequivocally that verse 26 refers to the destruction of Jerusalem in A.D. 70, then he is also *admitting* that there is a clear reference to the Temple as well, since there *was* a Temple that existed at the time of the A.D. 70 destruction. History has proven that the Temple did exist in A.D. 70, but was burned to the ground and even the very stones that were on top of one another were removed. This is historical fact. In insisting that the passage does not directly mention a Temple, he seems ignorant of the facts of history, yet he has no problem also unequivocally stating that the destruction of Jerusalem took place in A.D. 70. This is also when the Temple was fully destroyed as well. If he is stating that there is no mention of a rebuilt Temple of the future (from our vantage point), he still needs to prove that, not merely state it.

No Sacrificial System without a Temple

It is possible that Wohlberg means that there is no mention of a *rebuilt* Temple in these verses. The problem of course, is that there *is* mention of the sacrificial system. This system cannot occur outside of the Temple area proper. Synagogues cannot be used for this, so the text must be referring to the Temple proper. Wohlberg *makes the choice* to interpret this part of the text to mean that Christ Himself caused the sacrifices to cease through His death. However, this is not accurate, since the sacrificial system in Judaism continued until long after Christ's death. Wohlberg would undoubtedly say that Christ's sacrifice, being final, is the one God recognizes. Fine, but that does not really take care of the sacrificial system problem of the passage.

The real difficulty in the passage is the reference to the person that the use of the word "prince" (small "p") points to (as well as the pronoun "he" points to in the verse). Wohlberg believes that this "prince" is Titus; however, this is not instantly clear from the text, nor can it be proven without equivocation. The text says "*the people of the **prince who is to come**.*" If we know that the Romans destroyed Jerusalem and the Temple in A.D. 70, then all we really know is that this prince will either be merely their leader, or will be their leader *and* of the same nationality as the Romans; *Gentile*.

In essence, the angel Gabriel (who is sharing this information with Daniel), could just as easily be stating that the coming one-world ruler, known as the Antichrist, will be of the same stock as the people who will destroy the city and the sanctuary; *Gentile*, which took place in A.D. 70. However, Wohlberg chooses to believe that Titus is the "prince" who led the Romans to destroy Jerusalem.

However, in truth, *which* prince are we talking about here though? History indicates when the siege of Jerusalem *first* began (circa A.D. 66), General Vespasian led the troops, until he was called back to Rome. Then his son Titus took over. Has Wohlberg decided that the prince in Daniel must be referring to Titus simply because Titus *finished* the job his father began?

Actually, *two* individual generals took part in the destruction of Jerusalem and the Temple. By what standard are we to say that either man was really a "prince" when they were involved in attacking and destroying Jerusalem? Neither was actually a Caesar of Rome at the time, unless being a general equates to being a prince, but that seems a stretch to me. Vespasian *became* Caesar after he began to attack Jerusalem, which is the reason his son took over. If anyone should be noted as the prince in this passage, of the two, it would be best to declare Vespasian the prince, not Titus, since Vespasian became Caesar.

Who is "He"?
Verse 27 simply says, "*he will make a firm covenant for one week.*" This

needs to be thoroughly investigated before coming to any conclusions. Wohlberg has decided that this "he" refers to Jesus, and for him, there is no alternative. That is fine if Wohlberg has chosen to be dogmatic about it, but it is difficult to support his position, especially when considering the rules of grammar and the context of the passage itself. Let's take a closer look. Ultimately, Wohlberg is offering his opinion (as are the rest of us), and it is up to him to ensure that he provides enough evidence to support that position.

Regarding verse 27 – "and he will make a firm covenant for one week" – this is, I believe, the start of the 70th week, or the Tribulation. We will deal with why this is the start of the 70th week shortly. Regarding the use of the pronoun "he," it is determining who this refers to that makes or breaks this verse and its meaning.

Wohlberg looks to commentators like Henry, Clarke and J-F-B for proof of his position, all of whom share the same or similar points of view that Wohlberg does. Let's throw in at least one conservative scholar to mix it up. Arnold Fruchtenbaum points out *"The pronoun* he *in verse 27 goes back to its nearest antecedent:* the prince that shall come, *in verse 26. The* he *who makes a covenant in verse 27 and* the prince that shall come *are one and the same person, better known in evangelical circles as the Antichrist. The* prince that shall come, *or the Antichrist, will make* a firm covenant. *He will make it firm; he will make it strong. The Hebrew word does not mean to renew an existing covenant, but to make an original one containing strong guarantees. Exactly what it will guarantee will be made clear in the next passage."*[21]

Here is the section Fruchtenbaum is referencing: *"Then after the sixty-two weeks the Messiah will be cut off and have nothing, and the people of the **prince who is to come** will destroy the city and the sanctuary. And*

---

[21] Arnold G. Fruchtenbaum, *Footsteps of the Messiah* (San Antonio: Ariel Ministries 2003), 196

its end will come with a flood; even to the end there will be war;
*desolations are determined. And **he** will make a firm covenant with the*
*many for one week, but in the middle of the week **he** will put a stop to*
sacrifice and grain offering; and on the wing of abominations will come
one who makes desolate, even until a complete destruction, one that is
decreed, is poured out on the one who makes desolate." (emphasis
added)

Rules of Grammar: Antecedents
Fruchtenbaum's point is that the first use of the pronoun "he" in the
text (And **he** will make a firm covenant...), must of necessity be referring
back to the "prince who is to come" (the Antichrist), not Messiah. He
shows this by pointing out by following the rules of grammar, the
nearest antecedent from "he" is the "prince who is to come." By
definition, an antecedent is *"a word, phrase, or clause, usually a*
substantive, that is replaced by a pronoun or other substitute later, or
occasionally earlier, in the same or in another, usually subsequent,
sentence. In Jane lost a glove and she can't find it, Jane is the antecedent
of she and glove is the antecedent of it."[22]

In an attempt to clarify his position, Wohlberg published an additional
article titled "Daniel 9:27b Explained." Apparently, he had received
quite a few emails about his position, because it was not fully clear. In
my opinion, it is still not clear how he arrives at his position.

In the article, Wohlberg states, *"Grammatically, it makes sense that all*
references to "he" in Daniel 9:27 refer to the same person throughout
the text, that is, to Jesus Christ Himself."[23] Really? Does it? Obviously
Wohlberg and Fruchtenbaum cannot both be correct. There are at least
two individuals in the passage though. In verse 27, there are three uses
of the pronoun, *he.*

---

[22] http://dictionary.reference.com/browse/antecedent
[23] http://www.whitehorsemedia.com/articles/details.cfm?art=98

In verse 25, the angel Gabriel uses the title *"Messiah, the Prince"* (note capital "p"). In verse 26, Gabriel says *"Messiah"* will be cut off. Also in verse 26, we are introduced to a "people" and also a "prince" of those people (small "p"). It is immediately following this – in verse 27 – that Gabriel cites three uses of the pronoun, *he*.

He, Messiah, Prince – *Who?*

As stated, Wohlberg is certain that this prince was actually Titus, yet he also insists the "he" that refers *back to this prince*, is Jesus Christ. It cannot be. If the "he" being used (he *will make a firm covenant*), points to Jesus, then it would have been proper for Gabriel to say "Messiah the Prince" or "Messiah" again, because there has been an introduction of *another* character in between the use of the first Messiah the Prince. It should be obvious that the use of the pronoun "he" references not *Messiah the Prince*, as Wohlberg claims, but points to the "prince who is to come," whose *people* destroy Jerusalem. Note that the verse is really emphasizing the fact that it is the *people,* not the prince, who destroy Jerusalem. The prince is only part of the picture because he is likely of the same ethnicity, but will arrive on the scene later.

This prince (small "p"), cannot be referring to Titus in the first instance of use, and then the "he" immediately *after* refers to Jesus. This is why Wohlberg says that all three uses of "he" in verse 27 refer to Jesus; however, rules of grammar make this impossible.

Let us try it Wohlberg's way though: *"So you are to know and discern that from the issuing of a decree to restore and rebuild Jerusalem until **Messiah the Prince** there will be seven weeks and sixty-two weeks; it will be built again, with plaza and moat, even in times of distress. Then after the sixty-two weeks the **Messiah** will be cut off and have nothing, and the people of the **prince who is to come** (Titus) will destroy the city and the sanctuary. And its end will come with a flood; even to the end there will be war; desolations are determined. And **Jesus** will make a firm* *covenant with the many for one week, but in the middle of the week* **Jesus** *will put a stop to sacrifice and grain offering; and on the wing of abominations will come* **Jesus** *who makes desolate, even until a complete destruction, one that is decreed, is poured out on the one who makes desolate."*

This unfortunately makes no sense grammatically. The first use of "he" (where "Jesus" has been substituted), of necessity *must* refer to that closest antecedent, which is the "prince who is to come." It cannot be any other way, in spite of what Wohlberg and others *want it desperately to say*. Besides, if Gabriel was very careful to use the term "Messiah the Prince (capital "p"), followed by "Messiah" in the next instance, of which both refer to Jesus, why would Gabriel simply refer to Messiah as "he" in the last instance? It should be apparent that Gabriel chose the title Messiah deliberately, out of absolute respect for Messiah. Referring to Messiah, as "he" is without doubt, not as respectful. This is why Gabriel does not refer to Messiah as "he" when it would have been an obvious choice (after the first usage of "Messiah the Prince"), but continues to call him "Messiah."

Will This Help?

Put another way let's consider this example*: John and Paul worked in the warehouse and while Paul drove the forklift, John put the boxes on the shelves.* **He** *managed to finish his job in no time.*

In the above situation, there should be no confusion about who the "he" is referencing. We are introduced to both John and Paul and are told exactly what jobs they do in the warehouse. The last person mentioned by name is John. The sentence immediately following the last sentence containing the actual name of one of the individuals, contains the use of a pronoun. This pronoun of necessity (because of the rules of grammar), is pointing back to the very last person named. In this case, it is John.

It is the same exact situation with Daniel 9:24-27. Messiah the Prince is mentioned, followed by a reference to Messiah (which could have been "he" if Gabriel had wanted to say "he" instead of Messiah). These two are obviously the same individual. Immediately after this, we are introduced to "the people," and we learn that these people will destroy Jerusalem and the Sanctuary (or Temple).

Pronouns have a Job to Do
We also learn that these people are of the same ethnicity as the *"prince who is to come."* This is the introduction of another character. It is immediately *after* mentioning this particular prince that the text begins to use the pronouns. The possibility exists that Gabriel includes this prince to connect this prince with the ethnicity of the people who destroyed Jerusalem in A.D. 70.

The pronouns then, must of necessity point back to this *"prince who is to come."* That is how grammar works, in spite of Wohlberg's claim that *"Grammatically, it makes sense that all references to "he" in Daniel 9:27 refer to the same person throughout the text, that is, to Jesus Christ Himself."* No, grammatically, it does *not* make sense at all and Wohlberg should know better than that. If the pronoun "he" in all three cases refers to Jesus Christ, the entire text makes no sense whatsoever, in spite of Wohlberg's attempts to make the text fit his scenario. In fact, why did Gabriel even bother to include the phrase "of the prince who is to come" after "the people" if he was not intending to reference that particular character afterwards?

If what we have stated is correct about grammar usage, then the three uses of the pronoun "he" in verse 27 *cannot* be referring to Jesus Christ at all. Beyond this, if the three uses of the pronoun "he" refer back to the nearest antecedent, it would have to be the "prince who is to come." Wohlberg says this prince is Titus, which would mean that everything in verse 27 refers to Titus, yet Wohlberg insists that the use of "he" here refers to Jesus. This makes no sense at all.

Fruchtenbaum believes that the starting point of the seven-year Tribulation is yet future. It will begin with the signing of the covenant mentioned in the last portion of Daniel 9:24-27. Fruchtenbaum states, *"[the text] states that the covenant is made with many; not with all, but with many. The Hebrew text uses a definite article meaning the many. This is the leadership of Israel that will be empowered to sign covenants of this nature. The covenant is made for one seven. On one hand, it begins the seven years of the Tribulation, but on the other hand, it is also signed for the specific purpose of being in effect for seven years."*[24]

The text in Daniel tells us that in the middle of the week, the sacrificial system will be halted by this individual (the "he" mentioned in Daniel 9:27). This individual does this by breaking the covenant, and this breaking of the covenant is what causes the cessation of the sacrifices. Some "abomination" occurs and stops the sacrificial system. The rest of verse 27 refers to some type of abomination that spreads throughout the Temple area.

Since the sacrificial system is obviously in operation here, the Temple, of necessity, *must* be up and running. Wohlberg chooses to believe this is the Temple of Jesus' day. However, the text could be referring to a Temple that is yet to be built. Is this not exactly what Israel is attempting to do now, in 2010, and has been for some time?

A Temple in the Making
Israel has begun a full scale Temple just outside of Jericho. They will use this Temple to train priests for all aspects of their priestly duties. At the same time, all the furniture of the Temple has been built, as have all the

---

[24] Arnold G. Fruchtenbaum, *Footsteps of the Messiah* (San Antonio: Ariel Ministries 2003), 196-197

robes and even the altar, which was made portable enough to relocate once the real Temple is built in Jerusalem. For anyone who doubts this, all that needs to be done is head on over to the Temple Institute on the World Wide Web, to see all the preparations that Israel has been making for the past number of years. (http://www.templeinstitute.org/)

Fruchtenbaum explains, *"The word wing refers to the pinnacle of the Temple, and it is a Hebrew word that means 'an overspreading influence.' This overspreading influence will be upon the pinnacle of the Temple. This specifically refers to the worship of the Antichrist, when he declares himself to be the one true god (II Thes. 2:3-4). The word abomination in Hebrew refers to 'an image' or 'idol,' meaning that an image or idol of the Antichrist will be set up in the Temple Compound on the pinnacle of the Temple itself. This is also spoken of in Daniel 12:11 and Matthew 24:15. The image itself is spoken of in Revelation 13:14-15. "Upon the wing of abominations [upon overspreading influence of idol worship] shall come one that makes desolate."*

Here are two completely different versions of the same text of Scripture, Wohlberg's and Fruchtenbaum's. Which sounds more in keeping with the text itself, and which makes more sense? You decide.

Point 6 – Meaning of the Word "Covenant"
Wohlberg states that the use of the word "covenant" always references the Messiah. Specifically, he stated, *"The word "covenant" is Messianic, and always applies to the Messiah, not antichrist."*[25] He refers to Galatians 3:17 and Romans 15:8 to prove his point. I am not sure how Wolhberg arrives at this position actually. For instance, there are examples of covenants in the Bible, which have nothing directly to do with God. We see in Genesis 26:26 a covenant, which takes place between Isaac and Abimelech over the use of a well. God Himself has instituted a number of covenants with people like Abraham, Noah,

---

[25] http://www.whitehorsemedia.com/articles/details.cfm?art=33

Moses and others. These specific covenants did not necessarily reflect a Messianic nature. There is also the covenant between Jacob and Laban, found in Genesis 31.

The New Covenant, which is certainly hinted at in God's initial covenant statement with Abraham (Genesis 12:-13), is specifically Messianic in nature (cf. Isaiah 42 and 53; Jeremiah 31, 32, 33, 34; Malachi 3; Hebrews 13, 21; 1 Corinthians 11; and in each of the Gospels). Since Wohlberg has merely made a statement about all covenants being Messianic, but has provided nothing that would allow us to know exactly what he means, we are left to wonder. It is obvious from Scripture though, that not all covenants are related to Messiah.

Point 7 – Covenant Refers to Shedding of Christ's Blood
We have already discussed the meaning of "confirming the covenant with many." Wohlberg believes it refers to Christ's atonement, and also believes that in Matthew 26:28, Jesus is quoting Daniel directly. I would disagree here, stating that what Jesus is referencing is found in Exodus 24:8 (when Moses sprinkled the blood on the people as the sign of the covenant). The writer of Hebrews 9:20 refers to this same covenant.

In the Daniel text, there is absolutely no mention of **blood** associated with this covenant and one can only wonder why God would have left this extremely important part out, if in fact, the text in Daniel *does* refer to the cross of Christ.

Point 8 – "He" Will Cause Sacrifices to Cease
Wohlberg believes that "the middle of the week" points to the death of Christ. He states, *"After 3 ½ years of ministry, Jesus Christ's death put an end to all sacrifices in God's sight. He is the final Sacrifice!"* Here is where we see Wohlberg's use of allegory comes into play. In another article he wrote, Wohlberg speaks of the literality of the "weeks" of Daniel meaning "years." He also believes that Jesus' ministry lasted three and a half years.   Right after that (three and a half years), Jesus

was crucified. Can it be proven that Jesus' death came in the middle of this 70th week?

However, what does Wohlberg actually believe regarding the 70 weeks? In another two-part article titled "7 Years of Tribulation? Part 1," this is what he states about the period of the weeks found in Daniel 9: *"Thus we have a prophecy about "seventy weeks." Gabriel then subdivides the period into three smaller periods of seven weeks (verse 25), sixty-two weeks (verse 25), and one week (verse 27). 7+62+1=70.*

Seventy weeks = 490 days. **A day in prophecy represents a year** *(see Numbers 14:34 and Ezekiel 4:6). Thus 490 days are really 490 years. Without going into all the chronological details here (I will get more specific in a later chapter), the prophecy starts with a direct "commandment to restore and to build Jerusalem" (verse 25) after the Babylonian captivity and reaches down to the first coming of Jesus Christ. After 69 weeks (after 483 years), "shall Messiah be cut off" (verse 26). All Christian scholars apply this to the crucifixion of Jesus Christ. After our Lord's agonizing death, "the people of the prince that shall come shall destroy the city and the sanctuary" (verse 26)."* [26] (Emphasis added)

Neither the Numbers nor the Ezekiel passages, which Wohlberg references, represent a hard rule of days equaling years. In both cases, God was punishing Israel, and chose (because of their sin), to take the many years they had broken His law, and shrink it down to one day for each year. This should not be applied to prophecy uniformly.

Besides this, I am not clear here though. On one hand Wolhberg seems to be stating that the 69 weeks ended with the first coming of Jesus Christ. I am assuming he is referencing the First Advent, or His actual birth. If this is the case and if one "week" is really seven years, then how

---

[26] http://www.whitehorsemedia.com/articles/details.cfm?art=46

is it possible to go from His birth all the way through His life including His public ministry, and then state that "the middle of the week" is referring to Christ's death? This event occurred roughly 33 years *after* Jesus' birth. Wohlberg emphatically states that there should be no gap between the 69th and 70th weeks, yet he seems okay with the fact that there is actually a gap of about 30 years or so, according to his calculations.

Wohlberg is convinced no gap exists between these sets of weeks, yet his arithmetic leaves something to be desired, if I understand him correctly. Moreover, Wohlberg asserts that those of the early church never applied a seven-year period to a Tribulation. He comments, *"This may shock you, but historically, the vast majority of well-respected Bible scholars have not applied Daniel 9:27 to a seven-year period of tribulation at all. Neither have they interpreted the "he" as referring to a future antichrist (as many do today). Instead, they applied it to Jesus Christ."*[27]

No Surprise Here

No, in all honesty, this "revelation" does not shock me. If one considers the fact that it was not long after the last apostle died, that allegory began to force its way into the interpretive methods of the visible Church, then it can be understood why the Roman Catholic Church became such a big hit. Unfortunately, through people like Polycarp and Augustine, allegorizing Scripture became the normal mode of interpretation, especially in the area of prophetic discourse, and it has continued down through successive generations to today. The problem with automatically viewing Scripture allegorically is that the interpreter becomes the sole decision-maker with respect to the meaning of any given portion of Scripture.

---

[27] http://www.whitehorsemedia.com/articles/details.cfm?art=47

Interestingly enough, Wohlberg, a Seventh Day Adventist, espouses that the Roman Catholic Church is the "beast" of Revelation, with the pope as its head. Yet, he unfortunately uses the same techniques when interpreting passages on prophecy that Augustine and the Reformers utilized. Though Wohlberg's results are different from theirs, the truth of the matter is that allegory is found and heavily perpetuated in both camps. The Bible's meaning when it comes to prophetic discourse is essentially up for grabs when using allegory as the main interpretive took for Eschatology.

Once allegory was firmly in place, and Augustine had moved ahead with his views on certain things (regarding his anti-Jewish views, and in the area of Eschatology), the Roman Catholic Church began to develop in earnest. By the time of the Council of Nicea, the Catholicism was going nearly full bore. Over the coming centuries, more and more of orthodoxy morphed into something that was suited to Roman Catholic beliefs. We all know this all led to the *Reformation*.

The Reformation Gets <u>Salvation</u> Back on Track
While God obviously used Luther, Calvin, Zwingli and others to correct the wrongs done to the authentic Gospel and the true salvation found in Jesus Christ, other areas, which were just as wrong were left alone. Eschatology was one such area. This should tell us how a person believes regarding the End Times does not add or take away from his salvation.

The most important doctrine is that which is related to the only salvation available, and that is through Jesus Christ. The atonement of Christ is supremely important because if people do not understand that Jesus died on behalf of us, they will never recognize their need for a Savior to begin with. Moreover, other doctrines, which tie into the doctrine of salvation, are just as important; doctrines such as the deity of Christ, the virgin birth, the physical death, the physical resurrection and ascension of Jesus, the fact of the Trinity and a few others. These doctrines are non-negotiable, yet we see in the history of the Roman Catholic Church a perversion of many of these doctrines.

Changing the View

Satan wasted no time once the last apostle was gone, to begin to corrupt the truth of God. He did this first with individuals who saw the meaning of Scripture via allegory. While allegorizing Scripture, new interpretations came to the fore and these often pushed the true orthodoxy of the faith to the back burner, or off the stove altogether.

I do not believe that God raised up the Reformers to change anything with respect to Eschatology (the study of the End Times). It simply does not really matter and has no direct impact on a person's salvation. What matters is in the area of Soteriology (salvation), and the doctrines specifically connected to it. If a person gets this wrong, eternal life hangs in the balance.

It is incredibly important for people to have a right understanding of just who Jesus is, what He came to accomplish and whether His death, resurrection and ascension provide eternal life at all. This is what is most important. If people prefer to believe in a Pre-Trib, Mid-Trib, Post-Trib or no-Trib Rapture, their salvation is not affected. They are not somehow deceived if they believe in a PreTrib Rapture. If I am wrong about that belief, then I am merely wrong, not deceived. I could just as easily accuse Wolhberg of being deceived because in my opinion, his beliefs and arguments do not hold the muster.

Wohlberg's opinions do not stand up under the scrutiny of Scripture, in my opinion. Viewing the history of the Seventh Day Adventist movement clearly highlights many errant positions within the framework of their belief system. Since the movement itself began on the wrong foot regarding prophetic discourse, it is difficult to know how it can all of a sudden become correct in its beliefs.

If Wohlberg is wrong about his understanding, regarding the "he" points to in Daniel 9:27, then Wohlberg is actually stating that the Antichrist is *Jesus*. It appears to me as though he *is* deceived, solely because of the methods he uses to interpret, as well as the ramifications of his beliefs, with respect to not only Eschatology, but also regarding salvation.

This is at least part of the problem when people decide they are going to read the Bible for themselves and come up with their own theology. This is one of the tenets of Seventh Day Adventism, with William Miller insisting on it. People today believe that the Holy Spirit will teach everyone the correct theology, so they simply read the Bible, with no understanding of *how* to read it, and arrive at conclusions.

If certain rules are applied (essentially the same rules that we apply to all other forms of literature), we *should* all arrive at the same conclusions. We do not because we do not use the same methods. I wrote a book on this subject, which explains in detail aspects of interpreting Scripture.[28]

This is certainly not to say that the Holy Spirit cannot, nor does not teach us. He most certainly does, but to believe that the Holy Spirit is going to teach me the doctrines and then teach you the same doctrines, and then someone else the same doctrines, is to question why God has given teachers and pastors to the Church. If the Holy Spirit is in charge of teaching you, me and all the other Christians individually throughout the earth, then aside from fellowship, what is the point of attending a local church? What is the point of listening to a sermon? What is the point of reading a book on some aspect of theology? There is no point.

People proudly condemn those who believe in the PreTrib Rapture position for instance, because they accuse us of simply believing the

---

[28] See Fred DeRuvo's book, *Interpreting the Bible Literally (is not as confusing as it sounds)*, available at www.studygrowknow.com

Bible college professors, teachers and pastor who have delivered the message, but not proven their point.

These people also proudly point to the fact that they are renaissance men and women, apparently. They go directly to the Scriptures themselves to determine what the Bible teaches! Those poor souls who have adopted the PreTrib Rapture position have not done so, and have merely absorbed what has been told to them (snort!).

Point 9 – Overspreading Abomination

We have already dealt with this one. Unfortunately, we know from Wohlberg's own words that he does not equate this abomination with the event that Antiochus foisted upon the Jewish people in 168 B.C. In fact, Wohlberg makes no mention of it that I could find.

While Christ pointedly makes the statement *"Therefore when you see the ABOMINATION OF DESOLATION which was spoken of through Daniel the prophet, standing in the holy place (let the reader understand),"* Matthew 24:15 NASB). Jesus is obviously referring back to the book of Daniel and specifically referencing Daniel 9:27. When Matthew added, "let the reader understand," he was saying something cryptic yet it is only cryptic to us, if we do not possess knowledge of history prior to Christ.

Those of Jesus' day would have had no problem understanding what He had referred to with these words. The entire debacle of Antiochus was widely known by all. You could not be Jewish without having heard about this event as you grew up. The event refers to Antiochus having marched into the Holy of Holies, slaughtered a pig on the altar, sprinkled the blood around and demanded that the Jews worship him. This is a matter of recorded history.

Wohlberg's Understanding of the Abomination

Yet here is what Wolhberg says about the Daniel 9:27 text: *"'The abomination of desolation' (see Matthew 24:15) is not a simple subject, yet we know that Jesus clearly applied this event to the time when His followers were to flee from Jerusalem before the destruction of the second temple in A.D. 70. In a parallel text to Matthew 24:15, Jesus told His disciples, 'When you see Jerusalem surrounded by armies [Roman armies led by Prince Titus], then know that its desolation is near" (Luke 21:20, emphasis added). The disciples did 'see' those very events. Because of the 'abominations' of the Pharisees, Jesus told them, 'See! Your house is left to you desolate' (Matthew 23:38). Thus Gabriel's statement in Daniel 9:27 about Jerusalem becoming 'desolate' was perfectly fulfilled in A.D. 70."[29]*

So Wohlberg associates this "abomination" with the Pharisees. Does it sound to you like Wohlberg is guessing? From Daniel 12:11, we know that the length of time for this abomination to last will be 1,290 days. *"From the time that the regular sacrifice is abolished and the abomination of desolation is set up, there will be 1,290 days."* (NASB) Please note that Wohlberg does not mention this. He also does not mention the fact that 1,290 days is just over three and a half years, which places us just past the end of the Tribulation by thirty days.

However, with respect to the Matthew 24:15 passage, Fruchtenbaum states, *"This passage is merely a reminder of the Daniel prophecy, with no explanation as to what the Abomination of Desolation is. The only clue given is that it will be something* standing (like an image or idol), *in the Holy Place. This passage helps to verify the futuristic interpretation of the Daniel passage, for it was still considered unfulfilled and future at the time of Messiah. The Abomination of Desolation will serve as a warning to the Jews of Israel to flee the Land."[30]*

---

[29] http://www.whitehorsemedia.com/articles/details.cfm?art=47
[30] Arnold G. Fruchtenbaum, *Footsteps of the Messiah* (San Antonio: Ariel Ministries 2003), 253

In order to know if this Abomination of Desolation actually occurred during the A.D. 70 attack and destruction of Jerusalem, we need to ascertain whether Vespasian, Titus or anyone else for that matter, did what Antiochus Epiphanes did in 168 B.C. Interestingly enough, the history books (including Josephus) make no mention of any type of Abomination of Desolation. Even though the city of Jerusalem and the Temple were destroyed in A.D. 70, apparently, this Abomination of Desolation is yet to come, since we know it did not occur during this A.D. 70 attack. So it would appear that the Temple *is* going to be rebuilt in Israel. If so, there is an excellent chance that the Abomination of Desolation will also occur.

A Connection?

There appears to be a connection between the Daniel passage, the Matthew 24 passage, the Revelation 11 passage and what Paul refers to

2 Thessalonians 2:3-4

"Let no one in any way deceive you, for [the day of the Lord] will not come unless the apostasy comes first, and the man of lawlessness is revealed, the son of destruction, who opposes and exalts himself above every so-called god or object of worship, so that he takes his seat in the temple of God, displaying himself as being God," (NASB)

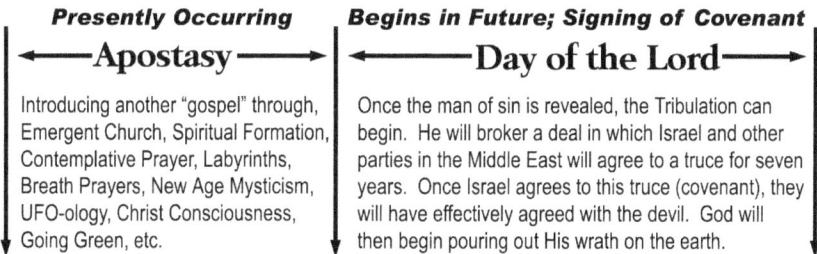

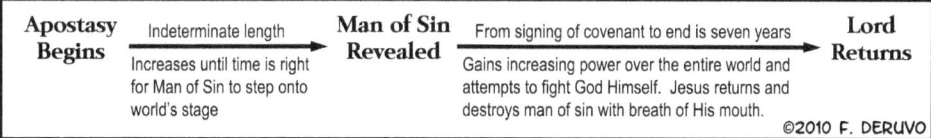

Presently Occurring	Begins in Future; Signing of Covenant
← Apostasy →	← Day of the Lord →
Introducing another "gospel" through, Emergent Church, Spiritual Formation, Contemplative Prayer, Labyrinths, Breath Prayers, New Age Mysticism, UFO-ology, Christ Consciousness, Going Green, etc.	Once the man of sin is revealed, the Tribulation can begin. He will broker a deal in which Israel and other parties in the Middle East will agree to a truce for seven years. Once Israel agrees to this truce (covenant), they will have effectively agreed with the devil. God will then begin pouring out His wrath on the earth.

Apostasy Begins	Indeterminate length → Increases until time is right for Man of Sin to step onto world's stage	Man of Sin Revealed	From signing of covenant to end is seven years → Gains increasing power over the entire world and attempts to fight God Himself. Jesus returns and destroys man of sin with breath of His mouth.	Lord Returns

©2010 F. DERUVO

63

in 2 Thessalonians 2:3-4. Paul is obviously pointing to a future, specific individual when he states the following: *"Let no one in any way deceive you, for it will not come unless the apostasy comes first, and the man of lawlessness is revealed, the son of destruction, who opposes and exalts himself above every so-called god or object of worship, so that he takes his seat in the temple of God, displaying himself as being God,"* (NASB).

Paul is stating that the Day of the Lord will not happen until:

- *"The" Apostasy occurs*
- *Man of Sin is revealed*

Once this apostasy occurs, and the Man of Sin steps onto the world's stage, *then* the Day of the Lord can begin. The Day of the Lord is normally viewed as the entire period of judgment known as the Tribulation. Please refer to chapter 14 of this book for a more in-depth discussion of the phrase "the day of the Lord."

Paul seems to be indicating that there is going to be one specific man at some future point who will literally sit in God's Temple, and declare himself god. This is a replication on a far greater level than even what Antiochus did in 168 BC! Wohlberg mentions none of this in his interpretation of the text. This is because he believes the pope to be the beast spoken of in the book of Revelation, and the Mark of the Beast is the changing of worship from Saturday to Sunday by the Catholic Church.[31]

This entire area seems convoluted, but if one considers the fact that within Seventh Day Adventism, the emphasis is placed on *works* regarding salvation, and then it begins to make sense. In the article noted above about the Sabbath Day, they also make this statement, *"The book of James tells us if we break one Commandment we have broken them all. So if the Sabbath is Saturday and if we are supposed to*

---

[31] http://www.sabbath-day.net/

be keeping the true Sabbath day then most Christians are guilty of breaking God's law. The Bible tells us that only a few will find the straight and narrow gate. Was this referring to Christians specifically?"[32]

Point 10 – Great Commission

Wohlberg states, *"Gabriel said that the 70-week prophecy specifically applied to the Jewish people (see Daniel 9:24). During the period of Christ's public ministry of 3 1 / 2 years, the Master's focus was largely upon "the lost sheep of the house of Israel" (Matthew 10:6). After His resurrection and then for another 3 1/2 years, His disciples preached mostly to Jews (see Acts 1-6). After that second 3 1/2 -year period, in 34 A.D., the bold Stephen was stoned by the Jewish Sanhedrin (see Acts 7). This infamous deed marked the then-ruling Jewish leaders' final, official rejection of the gospel of our Savior. Then the gospel went to the Gentiles. In Acts 9, Saul became Paul, the "apostle to the Gentiles" (Romans 11:13). In Acts 10, God gave Peter a vision revealing it was now time to preach to the Gentiles (see Acts 10:1-28). Read also Acts 13:46. Thus approximately 3 1/2 years after the crucifixion— and at the end of the 70-week prophecy given f or the Jewish people—the gospel shifted to the Gentiles exactly as predicted in Bible prophecy."*[33]

The above quote is interesting and it is why people like Wohlberg also believe that the Church has replaced Israel. To folks like Wohlberg, God is completely done with that nation, having finally and completely replaced her with the Church. While Jews of course, *can* become Christians, they become part of the Body of Christ, His Church. God no longer has any plans for Israel as a nation, but only Israelites as individual people.

However, Wolhberg's math needs to be checked here to see if he is even close to understanding the length of the full 70 weeks. On one hand,

[32] Ibid
[33] http://www.whitehorsemedia.com/articles/details.cfm?art=47

after explaining how he arrives at the total number of years found in Daniel 9:24-27 (490 years), Wohlberg makes this statement: *"After 69 weeks (after 483 years), "shall Messiah be cut off" (verse 26). All Christian scholars apply this to the crucifixion of Jesus Christ."*[34] Unless I am misunderstanding him, Wolhberg states that *after the 69th week has been completed, the Messiah is killed*. If he states that, then his other calculations are off. In other words, if the end of the 69th week arrives, and *then* Jesus is killed, I need to know *when* the 70th week begins. In fact, I need to know when the 69th week actually ended. Wohlberg does not say, as you can see.

Other scholars have done their own calculations and figured out that if they start with the decree to rebuild the Temple from Artaxerxes (cf. Nehemiah 2:1-8), and event that occurred in March 14, 445 B.C., it is simply a matter of counting forward from there. Sir Robert Anderson has figured out that from that date, moving 483 years into the future, we arrive at the day that Jesus entered Jerusalem triumphantly on the colt of a donkey. This would be approximately A.D. 32. If Anderson's calculations are correct, then this specific event of the Triumphal Entry marks the end of the 69th week. This then would be the fulfillment of the first and second groups of sevens found in Daniel 9:24-27.

As we know, it was a mere days later that Jesus was crucified. Yet, Wohlberg is stating that the first three and a half years of the final week of Daniel's prophecy (the 70th week), is Jesus' public ministry. However, as you can just see, the 69th week ended (according to Robert Anderson) with His triumphal entry into Jerusalem, where He presented Himself as King and was worshipped as such. This of course, infuriated the Pharisees. (Was there anything that did not infuriate them where Jesus was concerned?) How is it possible for Jesus to be cut off after the 69th week, and then turn around and count the three and a half years *prior*

---

[34] http://www.whitehorsemedia.com/articles/details.cfm?art=46

to the crucifixion as the first three and a half years of the final or 70th week, which would come *after* week 69 of Daniel's prophecy? This is what Wohlberg does, yet, this is the same person who tells us that everything in Scripture related to time is *consecutive*, and without stopping and starting. Then, why does he go backwards?

Confusing

If you will refer to the chart I have created, you will note the comparison between how I come up with the 70 weeks and how Wohlberg comes up with it. Please note that over his 69th week is also the 70th week, since to him, the first portion of the 70th week includes the public ministry of Jesus. This three and a half year ministry – he believes – takes us up to the midpoint of the 70th week, and the final three and a half years of the 70th week takes place in the book of Acts; Stephen's stoning, which Wolhberg states marks the ultimate and final rejection of Jesus by the religious authorities.[35] In fact, it was the crucifixion itself, which was the final and ultimate rejection of Jesus by the religious leaders of Israel.

Regarding the timing found in Acts, it is tricky to place an exact timeline for many of the events in the book of Acts. We know roughly, when things occurred, but to be dogmatically precise about all events is difficult at best.

For instance, we know that Paul's conversion to Christianity took place somewhere in the neighborhood of A.D. 33-36. We know that this event took place *after* Stephen was stoned to death. Paul's conversion *might* put us at A.D. 33. We do not even know exactly when Jesus was crucified. Our best guess is somewhere around A.D. 32, though some place it before and some after. If we add three and a half years past the crucifixion, we get to a date as early as the middle of A.D. 31 or as late as the middle of A.D. 33, possibly A.D. 34. Unfortunately, we do not

---

[35] http://www.whitehorsemedia.com/articles/details.cfm?art=47

483 Years of Prophecy
(of Daniel 9:24-27)

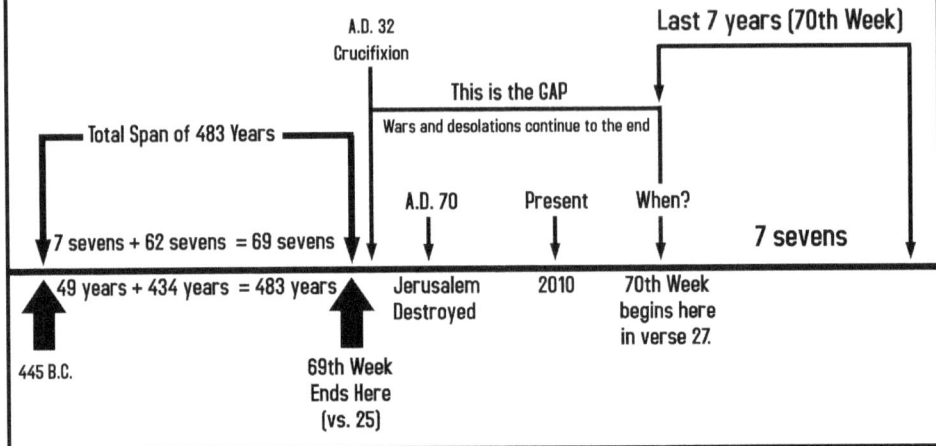

A.D. 32
Crucifixion

Last 7 years (70th Week)

This is the GAP

Wars and desolations continue to the end

Total Span of 483 Years

A.D. 70   Present   When?   7 sevens

7 sevens + 62 sevens = 69 sevens

49 years + 434 years = 483 years   Jerusalem   2010   70th Week
Destroyed   begins here
                                           in verse 27.

445 B.C.   69th Week
                        Ends Here
                        (vs. 25)

490 Years of Prophecy
(Wohlberg's Reckoning)

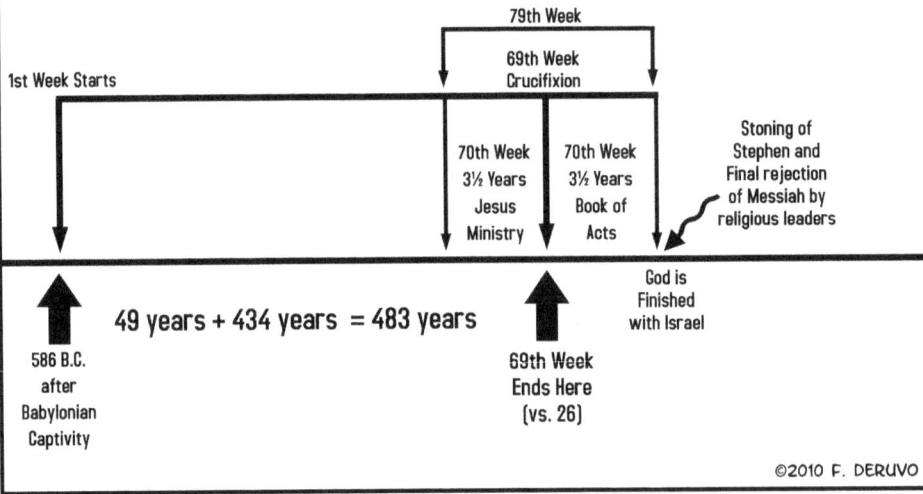

79th Week

69th Week
Crucifixion

1st Week Starts

70th Week   70th Week   Stoning of
3½ Years   3½ Years   Stephen and
Jesus   Book of   Final rejection
Ministry   Acts   of Messiah by
                                      religious leaders

God is
Finished
with Israel

49 years + 434 years = 483 years

586 B.C.   69th Week
after   Ends Here
Babylonian   (vs. 26)
Captivity

©2010 F. DERUVO

really know when Stephen was stoned to death, except that it was some time after the birth of the Church and the conversion of Paul.

Yet, in spite of this obvious variance, Wohlberg places exact spaces of two three and a half year periods; one during the public ministry of Christ and the second into the first part of the book of Acts. The only way to do this is to fudge the timeframes, or being willing to take an approximation as being *good enough*.

However, if we have a real starting date for the time the first set of seven sevens began, is there really a need to fudge anything? Moreover, if there is a GAP in the text of Daniel, would that not account for the fact that many today say we are not yet in the 70th week?

The Meaning of "Weeks"
In verse 24 of Daniel 9, Gabriel explains to Daniel that 70 weeks have been decreed for his people (the Jews). The word "weeks" should not have been translated weeks, but in the end, that is what they are though. Fruchtenbaum indicates that in the Hebrew, this word used for "weeks" here is *shavuim*, which literally means "sevens." In other words, it is very much like someone in America saying that he is going to buy a dozen. A dozen what? The word "dozen" is a modifier for either a noun or adjective. It indicates an amount, but not of *what*. Another word must be used for that. Say that you are going to the store to buy a dozen eggs is natural, and everyone understands that you are going to come back with 12 eggs, normally purchased in some type of cardboard container.

This is what Fruchtenbaum is saying about this word, "sevens." It simply is the *amount*, but amount of what is not necessarily known except within the *context*. For instance, consider a conversation that a wife is having with her husband:

Wife: Honey?

Husband: Yes.

Wife: Would you mind running to the store for me? I need a dozen eggs.

Husband: Sure, no problem. Anything else you need while I'm there?

Wife: No, just the eggs will work. Thank you.

Husband: Okay, I'll head down to the store and be back with a dozen in no time!

Off goes the husband to the store. Notice in the last sentence, spoken by the husband, all he did was use the word "dozen" but did not use the word "eggs" immediately following it. He did not need to clarify his meaning with the word "eggs" because the entire context of the conversation had to do with eggs from the start. The husband stated he would be back with a dozen and the wife knew that he meant a dozen eggs.

Context Often Flushes Out Meaning

It is the same thing with this Daniel passage. Gabriel is really saying that 70 *sevens* are decreed for his people, the Jews. How do we know to what the sevens refers? From the context. The entire context is speaking about *years*. Wohlberg goes through this interesting process of converting each week to days, then into years; *"Seventy weeks = 490 days. A day in prophecy represents a year (see Numbers 14:34 and Ezekiel 4:6). Thus 490 days are really 490 years."*[36]

We already mentioned that the two Scripture references do not connect to a hard rule about days to years. This is often what happens when people are prone to allegorizing Scripture. There is no need to do what Wohlberg has done, if the context is understood correctly. In some ways, it appears as though Gabriel was presenting Daniel with a bit of a

---

[36] http://www.whitehorsemedia.com/articles/details.cfm?art=46

play on words. Daniel believes (from reading Jeremiah), that the 70 years of captivity were almost over. Therefore, he sought the Lord and down came Gabriel. Gabriel is saying, *"No, Daniel, not 70 years, but seventy **sevens** of years."*

Verse twenty-five explains that these 70 sevens are going to be divided up. The math is 70 x 7 = 490. Since the context is dealing with years, we know that it is 490 years. The first section covers 7 sevens, or 49 years. The second section covers 62 weeks or 434 years. If you add 49 years to 434 years, you arrive at 483 years. This is just one week shy of the complete fulfillment of the 70 weeks.

Please note verse twenty-six. It begins with the words *"Then **after the sixty-two weeks** the Messiah will be cut off and have nothing."* What is Gabriel saying right there? He is saying that after the second division of sevens (or the 62 weeks) is finished, *then* the Messiah will be cut off, which is another way of saying that He will be crucified. The Messiah is said to have *nothing*. When Jesus died, he died naked and all had deserted Him, for fear of their own lives. The Father turned His own back on Him, as He poured out His wrath on Him, the wrath that should have been poured out on you and me. Jesus literally had nothing. He did not even have his own grave, but one was provided for Him by someone else.

Notice the text *then* states, *"and the people of the prince who is to come will destroy the city and the sanctuary And its end will come with a flood."* It is this agreed took place in A.D. 70; some forty years after Jesus died on the cross and is included in the Messiah being cut off timeframe. The end of verse twenty-six promises wars and desolations until the end. The end of what? The end just prior to the return of Jesus Christ.

The Gap
Now, we see that verse twenty-six begins with the words "Then after

this…" This is the break in the succession of weeks. The next (final, or 70th week), does not begin until we get to the text that states, *"he will make a covenant with the many for one week."* It should be obvious that because of what happens **between** the end of the 69th week and the beginning of the 70th, a break does exist. Between the first 7 weeks/49 years and the following 62 weeks/434 years, no break exists. However, *after* the 69th week has ended, we are told that a number of things will occur, one of which is the destruction of Jerusalem and the Temple, which we know happened in A.D. 70. It should also be clear that the final week of Daniel's prophecy does not begin until "he" makes a covenant with the many for one week. It is in discovering just exactly what this covenant is, that we are able to determine if it has already begun, or if it is yet future.

Though Wohlberg refers to it, he appears to ignore the A.D. 70 destruction of Jerusalem event in his *calculations*, preferring instead to go *backwards* to include the public ministry of Jesus (roughly three and a half years), and the very first part of the book of Acts (roughly three and a half years into it). At the same time, he complains that there is said to be a break or gap in the timetable, which he does not see, and claims that no place else in Scripture is there ever a break or gap in prophecy.

First of all, Daniel 9:24-27 is the *only* place that references this particular prophecy, so it is unfair to say that there cannot be a break here because there is never a break anywhere else (and we have already provided some evidence that would indicate otherwise). Second, though he thinks it is utter foolishness for this break to exist, he appears to have no qualms about jumping ahead to A.D. 70, but *not* counting it in the last week (70th week)! Therefore, on one hand, Wohlberg includes the A.D. 70 destruction as part of the *prophecy*, but does not include the additional 40 or so years in his *calculations*.

Please also note that beginning with verse twenty-seven, a covenant is made. Wohlberg points out that prophecy does not go out of order or stop and start. Yet this is precisely what *he* does in his attempts to make the text say what he wants it to say. If we simply read the text as is, we will find that these things happen in consecutive order (something that Wohlberg likes):

1. 7 weeks/49 years: Jerusalem is rebuilt
2. 62 weeks/434 years: ends with crucifixion of Jesus
3. The people (of the prince) destroy Jerusalem/Temple (A.D. 70)
4. Wars and desolations will continue to end
5. "He" will make a firm covenant with many
6. "He" will break the covenant in the middle by creating an Abomination
7. "He" will be destroyed

Everything noted above is sequential. They occur one after the other, yet Wohlberg jumps around, first going to the end of the 69 weeks with Christ's crucifixion, and then going *backwards* from that point to start the 70th week. But that is not what the text states or implies. It is a natural succession, with a break between the 69th week and the 70th.

The individual who comes along to make a firm covenant with the many is not Jesus Christ. Jesus made no firm covenant with anyone, except the Father. His covenant was written in blood, and because of that, *salvation is available to all*. The text indicates that the individual who comes along *will* enter into a covenant with the many. Jesus' covenant is with the Father. Christ has paid the full price of our sin. If we receive His salvation, then we also benefit from that covenant.

The last part of verse twenty-seven states, *"one who makes desolate, even until a complete destruction, one that is decreed, is poured out on the one who makes desolate."* What this verse is saying is that "one" will come and will make the Temple desolate. He will continue until his own destruction. How can this individual be Jesus Christ, yet it is the same individual that is in the beginning of verse 27.

In spite of the word play, Wohlberg's arguments simply do not stand up under the spotlight. Of course, you will have to decide for yourself if they stand up or not, but it appears as though they are severely lacking.

Understanding Daniel 9:24-27 is not at all that difficult as long as a few rules of interpretation are followed consistently throughout. The first is to note the *context*. The second is to avoid allegorizing, unless the text demands it. The third is to be consistent. The fourth, allow Scripture to interpret itself.

Wohlberg ends his two-part article on the Tribulation with a number of interesting comments. *"The entire 'seven-year period of tribulation' theory is an end time delusion, a massive mega-myth. It may even go down in history as the greatest evangelical misinterpretation of all time. The whole concept is like a gigantic bubble. Once Daniel 9:27 is correctly understood and the sharply-pointed pin of truth is inserted, 'Pop goes the seven years!' It's a fact: There is no text in the Bible which teaches a 'seven-year tribulation.' If you hunt for it, you'll end up like Ponce de Leon searching for the mystical Fountain of Youth, but never finding it."*[37]

The above comments of course, are merely Wohlberg's *opinion*, which he unfortunately presents as fact. This is why he never presents his views with the words, "In my opinion," or "It is my belief," or something similar. In *this* author's opinion, Wohlberg has done precious little to support his own opinions. There is an excellent chance that the seven-year Tribulation is not a delusion, or a giant bubble, nor will it pop. It is solely due to Wohlberg's interpretive methods, that *he* does not see the seven-year Tribulation, so to him it *is* a myth. That does not mean he is correct. It merely means that because of the way he has interpreted

---

[37] http://www.whitehorsemedia.com/articles/details.cfm?art=47

Daniel 9:24-27, he comes away with no seven-year Tribulation in sight. However, what if he is *wrong*? What if it *is* there and in his seeming arrogance, he is actually negating something that God has specifically placed in the pages of His Word? This is one of the biggest problems with presenting any type of biblical teaching. We are held to a higher standard...by God Himself. I believe I understand Daniel 9:24-27 correctly. I am also willing to say that I may be wrong.

One cannot help but notice that in spite of Wohlberg's extremely loose interpretive methods, he believes without hesitation that he has proven things beyond doubt. So strong in his beliefs is he that he ends his article, "The 70th Week of Daniel Delusion" with the words *"May error cease in our minds as we follow God's truth."* I could not agree more. If only Wohlberg could see his own error.

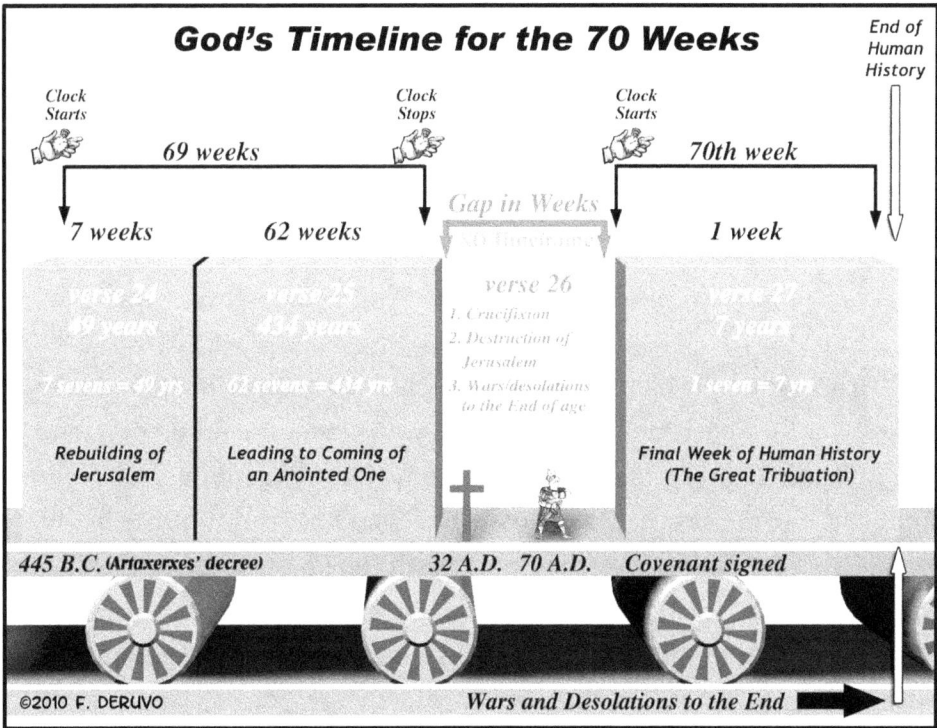

God's Timeline for the 70 Weeks

End of Human History

Clock Starts

69 weeks

Clock Stops

Clock Starts

70th week

7 weeks

62 weeks

Gap in Weeks

1 week

verse 24
49 years

verse 25
434 years

verse 26

1. Crucifixion
2. Destruction of Jerusalem
3. Wars/desolations to the End of age

verse 27
7 years

7 sevens = 49 yrs

62 sevens = 434 yrs

1 seven = 7 yrs

Rebuilding of Jerusalem

Leading to Coming of an Anointed One

Final Week of Human History (The Great Tribuation)

445 B.C. (Artaxerxes' decree)

32 A.D.   70 A.D.   Covenant signed

©2010 F. DERUVO

Wars and Desolations to the End

Chapter 3

Are You Prepared?

GRANDPA WAS NOT QUITE READY FOR THE
ADDITIONAL HORSEPOWER OF HIS NEW WHEELCHAIR

©2010 F. DERUVO

Part of the problem with people's misgivings regarding the PreTrib Rapture position has more to do with *their* perception of it, and unfortunately, they do not come by their perception of it honestly in some cases. Many Posttribbers and other anti-PreTrib Rapturists gain their understanding of both the Posttrib Rapture and PreTrib Rapture positions, from other people, not necessarily from the Bible only, even though this same charge is made against PreTribbers.

How many more times must we hear the constant claim that PreTribbers do not think for themselves, but merely take what they are taught by college professors or preachers, and go with that? This is honestly an arrogant position for anyone to hold, because it implies that only PreTribbers take the word of men along with, or juxtaposed against, Scripture. It is simply another way of stating that PreTribbers are not intelligent enough to think for themselves, so they are simply spoon-fed doctrine from preachers and teachers who delight in pulling the wool over other people's eyes.

However, in reality, all of us are guilty of taking the teachings of others and not investigating thoroughly enough. The Posttribber does it, the PreTribber does it – we all do it, and we need to be honest enough to admit that none of us is probably as thorough as the Bereans of Acts. So, for any of us to make a statement directed to another that they merely accept without conscience thought, what they are taught is certainly a bit arrogant. Aside from this, making a statement like that accomplishes nothing, except to put people on the defensive.

There are many manmade arguments out there for why the PreTrib Rapture position is false. Most of them can be easily rebutted; however, a rebuttal does not necessarily cause anyone to change their mind. While it might present them with a different view of the subject, it cannot convince anyone of anything. People will still be free to choose what they will and will not believe about the PreTrib Rapture.

Carnal, Lazy and Unspiritual
One of the more humorous reasons put forth as to why the PreTrib Rapture position is wrong, is due to the apparent belief that it creates Christians who are lazy, carnal, unspiritual, immature, and you could likely add your own adjectives to this list. At the outset, this appears to be a rather legitimate concern. After all, if the PreTrib Rapture position does reduce the spiritual level of Christians, then how can it be

Scriptural? However, is the problem with the doctrine itself, or people's understanding of that doctrine and supposed effect on people? If believing the PreTrib Rapture position causes me to sit on my couch, doing nothing except watching TV and life go by, then the situation must be investigated. Let us consider something at the outset though...some deny the eternal security of the believer because they say it tends toward licentiousness. Hey, if the tribulation is going to occur, I do not have to worry because the Rapture will save my skin from having to go through any real difficulties. Cool beans, I am good to go, literally!

Does anyone else see how this is purely a manmade argument, that really has no Scriptural bearing? The bottom line is this: is it the fault of God or the Bible if people take advantage of a doctrine because they have found what they consider to be a loophole in it? Hardly, yet that is actually what we are expected to believe, from the anti-PreTrib Rapture camp.

Easy-believism does not a Christian make. Yet many believe they are Christians because, at one point in time, they bowed their head (maybe even got on their knees), folded their hands in front of them, and prayed that Jesus would "come into my heart." *"There! Done! Cool, so let's get on with living, yeah!"* They rise up from their knees, head out the door of their church (or wherever they said this prayer), and soon afterward, fall right back into the pattern of living that they have always know, with nary a change anywhere that they can see.

Because of this though, the actual doctrine of eternal security of the believer is not disgraced. What *is* disgraced is how that particular individual understands the nature of salvation. Eternal security is an actual doctrine from Scripture, or it is not. If it is *not* a true doctrine, it is not due to a manmade argument.

If we look at Scripture, we will come to a parable in the Olivet Discourse that I believe strikes a death knell for any view of the Rapture, except the PreTrib Rapture view. It certainly resolves the problem concerning the possibility of the lazy and unspiritual person. This is the parable of the wicked servant, which begins in verse 44. Consider the text:

> 44 Therefore be ye also ready; for in an hour that ye think not the Son of man cometh.
> 45 Who then is the faithful and wise servant, whom his lord hath set over his household, to give them their food in due season?
> 46 Blessed is that servant, whom his lord when he cometh shall find so doing.
> 47 Verily I say unto you, that he will set him over all that he hath.
> 48 But if that evil servant shall say in his heart, My lord tarrieth;
> 49 and shall begin to beat his fellow-servants, and shall eat and drink with the drunken;
> 50 the lord of that servant shall come in a day when he expecteth not, and in an hour when he knoweth not,
> 51 and shall cut him asunder, and appoint his portion with the hypocrites: there shall be the weeping and the gnashing of teeth.

The verse reference numbers were deliberately left in for ease of reference. A number of things stand out in this parable, and one in particular, is the *attitude* of the evil (or wicked), servant. This particular individual servant became lazy and even started beating some of the other servants. Naturally, it needs to be asked what the reason was for the servant's despicable behavior. He lost sight of the fact that the Master of the house might return at any moment! In essence, not only did the evil servant stop *watching* (and therefore, expecting), the imminent return of the master, but he also apparently stopped *working*. From the narrative, it looks like he had plenty of time on his hands to sit around, fill his face with food and eat until he became drunk (cf. 49)! Hang onto that thought for a moment, while we go back to the Posttribber.

Imminency? What's that?

The Posttrib Rapture views says that *imminency* in the Scriptures does not mean "at any moment." Some of them say it means "soon." It does not mean soon at all and there is a huge difference between something occurring soon, and something being imminent. The word *soon* normally means that something will occur within a short period of time. The word *imminent* means that something could literally occur at any upcoming moment. For instance, we have heard the expression, "*If they don't get here soon, the food will be all gone.*" We understand that to mean that the food is going to run out within a short period of time and those who have been wasting time dilly-dallying getting to the event, will get none. This is quite different from saying, "*It looks like rain could be imminent.*" What that means is that it *may* rain (or not), and it *may* start raining at any moment (or not). We can look at the sky and attempt to judge it, but that is not a guarantee. We simply need to be prepared in case it does rain.

The evil servant showed his true colors when he began to doubt the master was ever going to return. It is actually the servants who *continued to believe* that the master could return at any moment, who continued to *work*, while they continued to *watch* for His return. In other words, these servants were very faithful to do what the master expected, even when he was not physically with them. It is very clear.

The fact that Jesus could return at any moment for His Bride is one of the greatest reasons to be working *while* watching. We should not be sitting around doing nothing when He returns! Those who think they have plenty of time, like the Posttribber, have every reason to sit on their rear, doing little to nothing, yet they accuse the PreTrib Rapture position of creating lazy, unspiritual, carnal Christians! The Scripture indicates that it is the exact opposite. Go figure.

In reality, the PreTrib Rapture position is the safest position, because it aligns itself with God's revelation through His Word. When comparing apples to apples, the other versions of the Rapture simply do not hold water. The timing of the Rapture is *unknown*, except that we know it will happen sometime before the Tribulation begins. It is precisely because of this, that we are to be constantly watching and constantly working. Doing anything else puts us in danger of becoming like the evil servant, and as we can see by reading the entire parable, things did not turn out well for Him.

Each day obviously brings us closer to the Rapture. However, will it happen in our lifetime? Only God, the Father knows the time that He has set, and He is not letting that secret out. In the meantime, we need to be watching and working, and we need to realize something else that is of more importance than the Rapture. While we are considering Scripture, and praying that as we study it, God will enlighten us regarding this area of Eschatology (the study of the End Times), or that area, we need to keep at the forefront of our minds one word: *eternity*.

Chapter 4

If the PreTrib Rapture is Wrong

Believing the PreTrib Rapture will save him from the coming tribulation, Larry gives up church, stops evangelizing and becomes a couch potato

HEY HON, WOULD YOU BRING ME SOME CHIPS AND SODA?

©2010 F. DERUVO

What must be understood is that I am not sitting here, simply *waiting* for the Rapture to occur, no more than I am simply waiting here for my death to occur. I *am* waiting, but I am *working* as well. My life continues because there are things that the Lord has for me to accomplish *until* such a time as He takes me home to Him, either through the Rapture, or my death.

Sometimes, we act as though we *know* that the Rapture and/or Tribulation are going to occur with the generation that is alive now. This thinking creates dogmatism. Because of this belief, things can get really heated in the arena of Eschatology. Accusations fly from one direction to the other, and we all react from the bur under our saddle, literally heaping abuse on one another.

Deceived, Sorry

Just this week, I was discussing this situation with a few individuals who happen to be Posttrib Rapturists. It was not long before I began to hear words like "deceived" being directed to me. No matter what I tried to say in my own defense – that I was not sitting around doing nothing, that I was actively seeking the Lord's will daily – none of it mattered. To these two individuals, I was deceived and that was that.

In fact, on a forum recently, this same notion was expressed to me like this, "*there is no such thing as a "rapture" the word isn't even in the Bible. Nothing even close to what people say about the calling up of the saved before the tribulation is even mentioned in scripture. Anyone who believes this is already in the hands of the antichrist and seem to wait joyfully for his arrival. Please go back and study to Word and know that there must be a falling away before and then a mass coversion (sic) to follow the antichrist. When the Temple is rebuilt and the antichrist goes in and declares himself to be God, then you will see the feet of our Lord land on Mt. Olive, Iron rod in hand, Justice will be served. God help those who choose to rapture up with the first whne (sic) they knew the Second will be Lord.*"

To this person, whose mind is completely set, not only is the PreTrib Rapture position untenable, but those who hold to that position:

1. We are already "in the hands of the antichrist," (whatever that means), and

2. We are filled with joy at the thought of the Antichrist coming on the scene

From his one statement alone, we can see his prejudices. First, he claims that the word "rapture" is not in the Bible. Is this true? From a hyper literal perspective, yes, he is correct. But how many times does this charge need to be responded to by those who believe and espouse a Pretribulational Rapture?

The word *harpazo*, in the Greek means, "a catching away," or "to be caught up." It is clear that Paul is speaking about a literal catching away, when the Lord calls His Bride home (cf. 1 Thessalonians 4:15-18). While the word "rapture" is not used, the clear *meaning* of *harpazo* provides us with the base word we use for Rapture.

The word "trinity" is not in the Bible either, yet that is what we *call* the doctrine referring to the Triune Godhead. There are any numbers of words and/or phrases, which are not in the Bible. They are named by individuals to represent a doctrine that *is* in the Bible.

Has anyone ever come across the word "eschatology" in the Bible? It means the study of last things, but the word itself is not in the Bible. Following this individual's logic then, we should not accept the doctrine of Eschatology either, due simply because the *word* is not in the Bible. It is a groundless argument foisted upon PreTrib Rapturists. It has no merit, yet used continuously as an argument that does have merit.

Prejudicial Leanings
The problem of course, is that many are prejudiced against PreTribulationalism because of the writings of Dave MacPherson. For many, the books that he has published represent the truth of the situation, that has been allegedly kept hidden for generations. Now, through his journalistic expertise, the conspiracy has been uncovered and made known. Because of this, there is no real need to go to the

Bible anymore, since the alleged truth has been made known about the origins of the PreTrib Rapture doctrine.

Nonetheless, where does this leave us? Since many have simply accepted and adopted as their own position, the teachings of Dave MacPherson, and the Bible is no longer needed to repudiate the PreTrib Rapture position, then discussing it is a waste of time.

Is it? If you are a PreTribber, you have undoubtedly heard this type of statements: *"The PreTrib Rapture is not in the Bible."* Maybe you've also heard this one *"I've heard all the arguments for PreTrib Rapturism and I can refute them all."*

As stated however, since Dave MacPherson has provided fodder for those opposed to the PreTrib Rapture position, then there is little point in discussing it. Since so many seem to be convinced that MacPherson has it correct regarding the PreTrib origins, it makes it even more difficult to discuss it intelligently because the PreTrib Rapturist is not only seen as wrong, but also wrong through deceit.

It's Like Talking to a Brick Wall
What can be done to convince people that there is actually merit in the PreTrib Rapture position? Ultimately, nothing, much like attempting to convince someone that Jesus Christ is God, the Son, who came to live, and eventually die on behalf of the sins of the world. His resurrection sealed our redemption, along with Satan's defeat.

What about discussing the doctrine of the Trinity with people who are convinced it is also a doctrine fabricated by men? It is difficult to get to any point of agreement, because of the way Scripture is understood by each individual. Not only this, but those opposed to the Trinity refer to the numerous councils of the church, most notably the Council of Nicea in which many state that the doctrine of the Trinity was virtually created at this meeting.

When all is said and done then, the only thing that can (and should) be done is to go to Scripture, and become a broken record, constantly repeating the *facts* found within God's Word. I do not believe for a moment that a necessarily wrong view of aspects of Eschatology condemns someone to hell. What condemns people to hell is their continued rejection of Jesus Christ – who He is, and what He accomplished on behalf of humanity. If they are wrong about salvation, then they are sadly, eternally wrong. This is tragic.

I continue to point to the Five Fundamentals of the Faith; those areas in which there is no wiggle room whatsoever:

1. *The Deity of Christ*
2. *The Virgin Birth of Christ*
3. *The Blood Atonement*
4. *The Bodily Resurrection*
5. *The Inerrancy of Scriptures*

The above five items are *not* negotiable. To be a Christian, by entering into a vital, living relationship with Jesus Christ, one must understand and believe that He is God, that He was born of a virgin, that the blood atonement was made possible through His death and that He was resurrected from the grave, and finally, that the Bible is inerrant.

Nowhere in the above do we see any reference to anything that is Eschatological in nature. There is nothing there which deals with the Last Days (or End Times), the second coming, the millennial reign of Christ, the Great White Throne Judgment, the eternal order of the future, or anything else even remotely referencing Eschatology.

So why is it we hear more and more people talking about the PreTrib Rapturist as being deceived and ultimately, an apostate? We see this because people superimpose their beliefs about the PreTrib Rapture doctrine, over and onto *salvation*. All manner of Scriptural gymnastics occur in attempts to show that *because* the PreTrib Rapture has a very questionable origin to say the least, then the results of believing and espousing it result in further error, and even deception. Because the New Testament speaks of the deception that is to occur during the End Times, resulting in a great apostasy, then it stands to reason that the PreTrib Rapture – with dubious and even deceptive origins – is necessarily part and parcel of that deception leading to the great falling away, at least according to some.

But *is it?* When Paul or Peter, or even Christ discuss or refer to the End Times and the deception, which will occur, what is the *actual context* of their meaning? In other words, what do they actually mean regarding *the* deception leading to the great falling away?

In order to understand that, we must look to a number of things that have been occurring within the visible Church today. These things continue unabated and create the situation, which is primary in causing this falling away. Is the PreTrib Rapture part of it? One thing is certain; all the things that I will discuss now have at their root, the same error. This error, I believe, is the error that leads people down the primrose path to destruction. Many of these individuals are regular church attendees. However, sadly they are not authentic Christians, but merely think they are Christians.

THE TRUTH, ACCORDING TO THE ANTI-PRETRIB RAPTURIST...

©2009 F. DERUVO

The poor, unsuspecting Bible College student goes into college as a free-thinking individual...

BIBLE COLLEGE IS GOING TO BE WONDERFUL!

...only to exit as an indoctrinated, robot, simply parroting the things they were taught while there.

THE PRETRIB RAPTURE...

THE RAPTURE IS PRETRIB!

Chapter 5

The Emergent Church

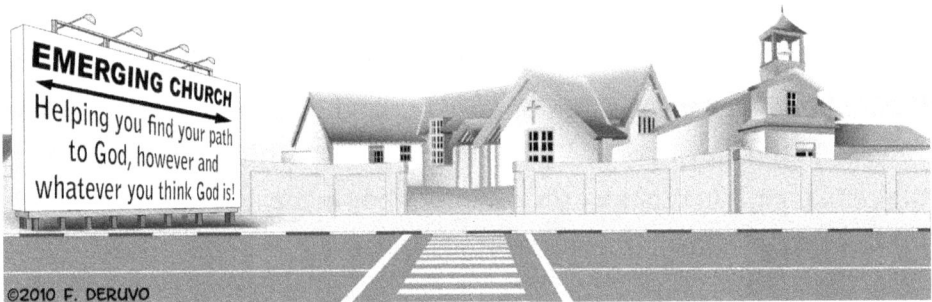

EMERGING CHURCH
Helping you find your path to God, however and whatever you think God is!

©2010 F. DERUVO

One of the biggest problems attacking the visible Church today (from within!), is found in the Emergent Church. Proponents of this movement see worship as one huge *conversation*. There is no one answer, because the answer might be different for everyone. Christianity is no longer "one size fits all." It has been broken down into parts and people are free to include one part or another; whichever fits into their particular lifestyle. The Bible is not viewed as being the final authority and in fact, people are encouraged to investigate other religious systems, which can then be incorporated into Christianity (if that were possible).

Some of the leaders in this movement are Tony Campolo, Tony James, Rick Warren, Dan Kimble, Brian McLaren, Leonard Sweet, and others who teach people to toss their antiquated views of Christianity and even Jesus Himself. They are encouraged to adopt a more modern – or even postmodern – mantra, in which all become one, and all roads once again wind up leading to God.

One of the keys to the Emergent Church philosophy is that Jesus Christ is not necessarily God, or at least, not the *only* representation of God. Some teach that Jesus can be found through Buddhism, or the New Age movement itself. In other words, though for ages, Christianity has been seen as alone unto itself, it is now being forced to receive other religious philosophies that are not in harmony with it.

There have been a number of excellent books published, which serve to enlighten the average person on the dangers of the Emergent Church. Check the resources at the end of this chapter for more information.

People like Brian McLaren have made statements like *"Christianity is too limiting."*[38] McLaren is one who emphasizes the need to expand the borders of Christianity so that aspects of other spiritual movements might be incorporated into it.

According to the folks at Lighthouse Trails Research Project, a number of important concepts are incorporated into Christianity, making it anything but Christian:

*"1. **You can keep your own religion** — Buddhism, Islam, Hinduism, you just need to add the biblical Jesus to the equation. Then you become complete. You become a Buddhist with Jesus, a Hindu with Jesus, a Muslim with Jesus and so on.*

---

[38] http://www.lighthousetrailsresearch.com/emergingchurch.htm

*2. **You can throw out the term Christianity** and still be a follower of Jesus.*

*3. In fact, you **can throw out the term Christian too**. In some countries, you could be persecuted for calling yourself a Christian, and there is no need for that. Just ask Jesus into your heart, you don't have to identify yourself as a Christian."*[39] (Emphasis added)

The above is essentially the Emergent Church's mission statement, which seeks to attract people to something far less constrictive than Christianity. In other words, though at times they will use the term Christian and Christianity to get people in the door, they will phase these terms out, going for terminology that is far more inclusive.

One large church just down the street boasts that their church is for people who do not like church. After having attended that church for some time, it is easy to see why people enjoy it. There is a coffee shop on the "campus," sermons are light enough to be entertaining, but not heavy enough to convict or teach. Rarely if ever, is the concept of sin or hell mentioned. This makes people feel uncomfortable, and – God forbid – *judged*. People who feel judged stop attending, and stop *giving*.

While the pulpit has been pushed to the side, in favor of a stool, or music stand, the pastor (such as he/she is), engages the congregation (audience) with large doses of humor. Very little Scripture is used in a "talk," and Scripture that is used, is used sparingly, so as not to ruin the flavor of the event.

Normally, the music is very upbeat and *loud*. In fact, the louder, the better. Loud, rock music breaks down people's inhibitions. People are encouraged to sway or move, and even clap their hands and shout in the raucous musical environment. Often there seems to be little (if any) difference between a live rock concert and this type of church service.

---

[39] http://www.lighthousetrailsresearch.com/newmissiology.htm

Making Church Huge

The Emergent Church is primarily about church *growth*. Get people into a building and then keep them there through entertainment. Short plays or full-length dramas, professional singers and musicians, fast-paced slide shows and more keep things moving for people in this video game generation. Before you know it, the event (church) is over, people head home, loudly proclaiming how much they enjoyed being in "church."

In truth, there is very little (if any) authentic Jesus in the Emergent Church movement. Proponents of the Emergent Church speak of being involved socially, while remaining whatever you are – a Buddhist, a humanist, an atheist, a theist, or whatever. All should come together to work for the common good of all humankind. This is what God wants, we are told. This is what God endeavors to accomplish through us, and in order for that to occur, barriers between the various religions must be broken down.

Why can't a Muslim worship with a Christian or Buddhist worship with a Catholic? The Emergent Church says there is no reason that they cannot, or should not worship together as one body. The differences have kept people apart for too long and they must cease.

I believe the Emergent Church is one of the movements, which is creating an environment of *apostasy* for the visible Church. Many are being indoctrinated by its principles and, interestingly enough, discussion of all things is greatly encouraged, except *Eschatology*. Don't go there. Why? Because it is divisive.

So here, we have a movement, which professes at least on the surface to be Christian, yet repudiates much of orthodox Christianity, in favor of a *conversation*. This conversation is supposed to make people feel more at home, more comfortable in church. It is supposed to increase the chances that people will not only come to church, but will *stay* in church.

The problem of course, is that the Emergent Church is something that God considers anathema. It is not something that supports who He is, or what He is accomplishing in this world. In that sense, it is diametrically opposed to God and His purposes.

Ousting Christ

What the Emergent Church encourages, is ultimately the reduction of Christianity and of Jesus Christ. It seems that the Orthodox Church has had it wrong for centuries. Okay, sure, Jesus is God, *however*, He is not the *only* way to the Father and that is not what He meant when He said that He was the way, the truth and the life (cf. John 14:6). We are told He meant something far greater, something far less restrictive.

The Emergent Church pulls people away from Jesus because of their abject refusal to *believe* and *espouse* the orthodox truths of Christianity. Through the Emergent Church, people are being drawn away by leaders who have an outward appearance of religious truth, but no power. The power is the power that *saves* people from hell. The religious leaders found within the Emergent Church are empty graves, whitewashed sepulchers, because they themselves do not have salvation, and they keep others from receiving it as well.

The fruit of the Emergent Church is found in its *results*. While large churches have become noticeable everywhere, what is being taught as well as omitted, is just as noticeable. These churches boast of their size, due to the number of those who attend. However, they are busy propagating error, by either omission or commission. They leave the Jesus of the Bible behind, or out of the picture entirely, in favor of promoting the '*conversation*' that promises no answers, nor provides any.

The Emergent Church is creating an atmosphere of confusion as it leads people away from Jesus and away from the only salvation that is available to them. The leaders of the Emergent Church could care less because they are too busy building their little kingdoms and making themselves the gods of this world.

The Message of Our Cover

This book's cover is deliberately created to focus on the fact that within our world, many things are working together to create a modern day Tower of Babel. This Babel, unlike the one in Genesis 11, is of a spiritual nature primarily. People are reaching out to the spiritual like never before and whether it is through something that resembles the church, or the New Age movement, people want their spiritual void filled. Note that on many girders, or floors of the building being constructed on the cover, are terms like *Spiritual Formation, Emergent Church, Dominion Theology* and more. The pieces are fitted together to create something that all can be involved in, to some degree or another, and in many cases, the need to be an authentic Christian does not even come into play, and is frankly, discouraged.

If people, who profess Christianity, would step back for a moment and attempt to see how all of these things are interacting, including overt New Age thought, they might realize that they are being taken for a ride by the powers of darkness. If you look closely enough at our cover, you may even note a few other things that are not as obvious at first, which are also playing a big part in the coming world order. These things are paving the way for the one-world system. Yet, in spite of this, many of those within Christendom act as if the PreTrib Rapture is the real (or sole) culprit (as noted by the group of men on the back cover). We have included an illustration on the next page, which highlights the process that we believe is happening in the world now. This same illustration is included twice in this book, once here and once further on in chapter 17 for good measure.

Lighthouse Trails Research Project has been on the forefront issuing warnings regarding the Emergent Church and its offshoots. In a recent emailed newsletter, they indicated that even the secular news is now announcing the fact that more professing Christians are incorporating aspects of Eastern Mysticism and the New Age Movement into what has always been Orthodox Christianity. The article from USA Today, written by Cathy Lee Grossman, reads in part, *"The chances are that one in five of the people there find "spiritual energy" in mountains or trees, and one in six believe in the "evil eye," that certain people can cast curses with a look — beliefs your Christian pastor doesn't preach."*[40]

Grossman goes on to say, *"Elements of Eastern faiths and New Age thinking have been widely adopted by 65% of U.S. adults, including many*

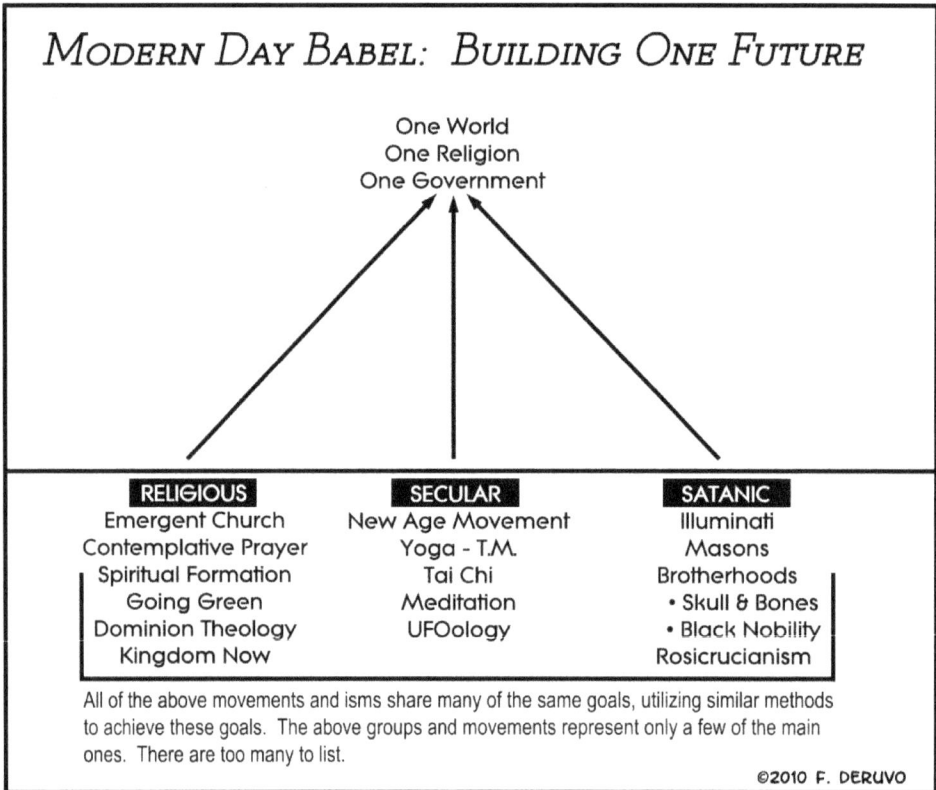

MODERN DAY BABEL: BUILDING ONE FUTURE

One World
One Religion
One Government

RELIGIOUS	SECULAR	SATANIC
Emergent Church	New Age Movement	Illuminati
Contemplative Prayer	Yoga - T.M.	Masons
Spiritual Formation	Tai Chi	Brotherhoods
Going Green	Meditation	• Skull & Bones
Dominion Theology	UFOology	• Black Nobility
Kingdom Now		Rosicrucianism

All of the above movements and isms share many of the same goals, utilizing similar methods to achieve these goals. The above groups and movements represent only a few of the main ones. There are too many to list.

©2010 F. DERUVO

---

[40] http://www.usatoday.com/news/religion/2009-12-10-1Amixingbeliefs10_CV_N.htm

who call themselves Protestants and Catholics, according to a survey by the Pew Forum on Religion & Public Life released Wednesday."[41] Of course, the tragedy is that people are being deceived into thinking that aspects of Eastern mysticism have anything to do with Christianity, and can therefore, be incorporated into it without damaging the real, true message of Christianity. Sadly, those who are so intent upon pointing the finger at those who believe and espouse the PreTrib Rapture seem not to be as bothered by the manifestation of these New Age elements within mainline churches, as much as they feel called to condemn the PreTrib Rapture position.

Eternal Security?

In communicating with someone via email, I mentioned that while discussing Eschatology (the study of End Times), has its place of importance, it should not override, or become greater than other areas of theology, especially salvation. This person believes in Lordship salvation and rejects eternal security, believing that Christians *can* lose their salvation. This is an area of far greater theological importance than studying or discussing aspects of the End Times.

While he believed salvation certainly was important, he felt Eschatology was as well, and then proceeded to delve into areas related to the End Times. For me, this is a huge problem, because this type of thinking is underpinned with the notion that a wrong view of Eschatology can or will affect someone's salvation. I do not find this in Scripture. I don't see this as ever being a condition for salvation, anywhere in the Bible.

We know of course, that Judaizers attempted to win converts to Judaism by stressing their obedience to aspects of the Law, like circumcision. However, Paul fought valiantly against this error, because to cave into the demands of the Judaizers would mean a turning away from the

---

[41] http://www.usatoday.com/news/religion/2009-12-10-1Amixingbeliefs10_CV_N.htm

Gospel. Paul certainly did not believe this to be possible, but it was a warning he needed to voice and voice loudly and clearly.

Regarding the article in USA Today, Lighthouse Trails newsletter comments on Grossman's note regarding 65% of U.S. adults have adopted New Age thinking, by stating, *"The implications of this are that we indeed are living in a time of departing, of which II Thessalonians 2 speaks. There is no turning back. This is a reality that we will be living with from now on. And it is the responsibility of biblical believers everywhere to be fully equipped in knowing how to counter this reality so that friends, loved ones, pastors, professors, and co-workers etc. can be warned."*

It seems clear enough. The End Times includes a serious, global falling away from the faith. Since I strongly believe the Bible teaches eternal security for each and every believer, what could Paul possibly be referring to when he states, *"Let no man deceive you by any means: for that day shall not come, except there come a falling away first, and that man of sin be revealed, the son of perdition,"* (2 Thessalonians 2:3 KJV)?

Apostasy, <u>then</u> the Man of Sin
Paul seems to be stating that before the man of sin is revealed, there must first be a falling away. This falling away could easily refer to those individuals who are merely *professing* Christians, but not authentic Christians. They have a *form* of religion, but the new birth has not taken place within them. This spiritual transaction has not been accomplished.

We already know from one of Christ's parables that as soon as the Church began, Satan wasted no time in sewing *weeds* (referred to as "tares" in the passage), which for all intents and purposes, looked very much like the wheat that had originally been planted by the landowner. Since tares and wheat look very similar, the landowner told the workers to wait until the harvest to separate the wheat from the tares (cf. Matthew 13). Then, they would not accidentally pull up wheat.

The text from Matthew 13 states, *"Another parable put he forth unto them, saying, The kingdom of heaven is likened unto a man which sowed good seed in his field: But while men slept, his enemy came and sowed tares among the wheat, and went his way. But when the blade was sprung up, and brought forth fruit, then appeared the tares also. So the servants of the householder came and said unto him, Sir, didst not thou sow good seed in thy field? from whence then hath it tares? He said unto them, An enemy hath done this. The servants said unto him, Wilt thou then that we go and gather them up? But he said, Nay; lest while ye gather up the tares, ye root up also the wheat with them. Let both grow together until the harvest: and in the time of harvest I will say to the reapers, Gather ye together first the tares, and bind them in bundles to burn them: but gather the wheat into my barn,"* (Matthew 13:24-30 KJV).

Christ is explaining in parable form how the evil one (Satan) would immediately seek to destroy what God was creating in the Church. Christ warned that Satan would do this by *imitation*. He sowed seeds that sprouted alongside the wheat, the good crop. Because of the similarity between the wheat and tares and due to the close proximity of the two, it would be far too dangerous for the workers to go into the fields while both plants were growing and attempt to separate them then. It would have to wait until the harvest, when everything would become patently clear and would be impossible for the "reapers" to make a mistake.

Real or Memorex®?

Many within the visible Church today are merely *imitators*, or *professors*. They do not know Jesus Christ, because they have not, through faith entered into a relationship with Him. Now, it is true that at least some of these that appear to be "tares" *may* wind up not being tares, but are actually individuals who *will* eventually come to Christ, entering into a living, vital, and viable relationship with Him, by faith. It is impossible to go through each local body, and attempt to determine who is, and who is not officially saved. Moreover, it is equally impossible to go through each local body and try to figure out who is a tare and who is wheat, and frankly, that is not the Christian's job.

It is because of the fact that the visible Church is filled with people who are tares that the Church experiences the types of divisions it does experience. Beyond this, the sin nature, which is still resident within each believer, plays a hand in creating problems in the visible Church, even among the "wheat." While Christians can make mistakes, and appear to fall back into the world, only Christ knows if they are *actual*, or merely *professing* Christians. If an authentic Christians falls backwards, do they lose their salvation? Not according to the Bible I am familiar with, however, they certainly lose *fellowship* with God through Christ, until such a time as they repent (confess their sin and turn from it), and do what they can to make things right.

Paul's emphasis in the 2 Thessalonians passage is on those who completely fall away from the faith. Therefore, in these last days, we can expect a large multitude of individuals who appear to be authentic Christians because of their association with their local church, fall away from the truth; the truth which they never really possessed from the start.

Repentance Does Not Always Lead to Salvation
I believe that it is possible to *repent* and *not* become a Christian. In other words, when a lost person repents, their opinion about Jesus changes. When faced with the question of who Jesus Christ is, there are only two choices. We either reject or accept the truth about Him. In rejecting the truth, we may again face that same question later on in life. God will continue to provide us with opportunities to change our mind (or repent), about Jesus. It is possible to repent – to change an

opinion about Jesus Christ – *without* that repentance leading the person to salvation.

I do not want to get into the debate over Lordship Salvation vs. Easy Believism. I also realize that by defining repentance as I have, some will object to it. The plain truth of the matter is that if we understand the biblical definition of repenting, it clears up a good deal of mystery.

Charles Ryrie states this about biblical repentance: *"The New Testament usage of* repentance *can be separated into three categories. First,* there can be a repentance that either has no relation to eternal salvation or at least does not result in salvation. *This may be labeled nonsaving repentance. It is not superficial, and it has a result or effect, though not salvation...Second,* there is a repentance that is unto eternal salvation. *What kind of repentance saves? Not a sorrow for sins or even a sorrow that results in a cleaning up of one's life. People who reform have repented; that is, they have changed their minds about their past lives, but that kind of repentance, albeit genuine, does not of itself save them. The only kind of repentance that saves anyone, anywhere, anytime is a* **change of mind about Jesus Christ**. *The sense of sin and sorrow because of sin may stir up a person's mind or conscience so that he or she realizes the need for a Savior, but if there is no change of mind about Jesus Christ there will be no salvation."*[42] (Emphasis added)

Of course, there are many who disagree with Ryrie about the concept of repentance. Some believe that unless there is a strong reaction against sin in a person's life, allowing that person to sense the weight of his sin, there can be no true repentance. If you do not experience a crushing of the soul due to sin's evil nature, then repentance has not occurred.

In Acts 2, Peter preaches the first sermon immediately following the birth of the Church. In it, he tells his listeners that they must repent.

---

[42] Charles C. Ryrie, *So Great Salvation* (Chicago: Moody Publishers 1997), 83, 85

However, about *what* are they supposed to repent? If we carefully read the biblical text, we should be able to see that Peter is telling them to repent, or *change their mind*, about Jesus Christ. In fact, his entire sermon is about Jesus Christ and the fact that He was crucified *because* people did not believe Him. Ryrie adds, *"Upon hearing and realizing [the truth of Peter's sermon], conviction overwhelmed the people. They asked what they should do, and Peter replied, 'Repent.' Repent about what? Change your minds about Jesus of Nazareth. Whatever you thought about Him before or whoever you thought He was, change your minds and now believe that He is God and your Messiah who died and who rose from the dead. That repentance saves."*[43]

In other words, it is impossible to receive salvation, unless we have a right understanding concerning the identity of Jesus Christ. Most of unsaved of the world believes Him to be, either:

- *A good man, a teacher, but not God, or*
- *A legend or a myth; someone who never lived.*

Many so-called Christians have a difficulty with this as well. Unless a person does a complete 180-degree turn, rejecting their false notions about Christ, to see and receive the truth about Him, salvation cannot occur. This first step – *repentance* – is the necessary prelude to receiving salvation. However, even in that, realizing the truth of who Jesus is does not provide salvation in and of itself. Understanding the truth about Jesus Christ puts us in the position of being *able* to receive salvation.

Ryrie again, *"Certainly when one changes his mind about Christ and receives Him as Savior, changes will follow in his life. All believers will bear fruit, so changes will follow."*[44]

---

[43] Charles C. Ryrie, *So Great Salvation* (Chicago: Moody Publishers 1997), 86
[44] Ibid, 89

Is repentance then, part of the process of salvation? Ryrie responds with, *"Yes, if it is repentance or changing one's mind about Jesus Christ. No, if it means to be sorry for sin or even to resolve to turn from sin, for these things will not save."*[45]

If we consider Judas, he betrayed Jesus into the hands of the religious leaders of Israel. Whatever his reasons were, he deliberately turned Jesus over to those who wanted Him dead. Afterwards, when he saw what was happening to Jesus, he *repented*. In other words, he changed his mind about his own actions, but that did not get him to the point of being able to receive salvation.

Ryrie again, *"Repentance and faith can be understood as 'two sides of the same coin'"* It is impossible to place your faith in Jesus Christ as the Savior without first changing your mind about who He is and what He has done. Whether it is repentance from willful rejection or repentance from ignorance or disinterest, it is a change of mind. Biblical repentance, in relation to salvation, is changing your mind from rejection of Christ to faith in Christ.*

"It is crucially important that we understand repentance is not a work we do to earn salvation. No one can repent and come to God unless God pulls that person to Himself (John 6:44). Acts 5:31 and 11:18 indicate that repentance is something God gives—it is only possible because of His grace. No one can repent unless God grants repentance. All of salvation, including repentance and faith, is a result of God drawing us, opening our eyes, and changing our hearts. God's longsuffering leads us to repentance (2 Peter 3:9), as does His kindness (Romans 2:4).

"While repentance is not a work that earns salvation, repentance unto salvation does result in works. It is impossible to completely change your mind without that new mindset causing a change in action. In the Bible,

---

[45] Charles C. Ryrie, *So Great Salvation* (Chicago: Moody Publishers 1997), 86

repentance results in a change in behavior. That is why John the Baptist called people to 'produce fruit in keeping with repentance' (Matthew 3:8). A person who has truly repented from rejection of Christ to faith in Christ will give evidence of a changed life (2 Corinthians 5:17; Galatians 5:19-23; James 2:14-26). Repentance, properly defined, is necessary for salvation. Biblical repentance is changing your mind about Jesus Christ and turning to God in faith for salvation (Acts 3:19). Turning from sin is not the definition of repentance, but it is one of the results of genuine, faith-based repentance towards the Lord Jesus Christ."[46]

Back to Paul and Thessalonians

Regarding Paul, what is most interesting about his comments to the Thessalonian believers is that at first glance, he appears to be saying that the people who fall away will fall away, *out of* the local church. A closer look reveals that they are falling away from the *Truth*, which is only found in Christ. He says nothing about them physically leaving the visible Church itself. It appears there will be more and more people who will leave one particular church (building), to find another one, which caters to their itchy ears. As far as they are concerned though, they are still "in church," and as far as the world sees, they are still "in church."

This is what makes Paul's words so dramatic. Today's churched society is placing a greater emphasis on all aspects of the Emergent Church. People are being carried away by the error that runs rampant throughout the *visible* Church today. The saddest part is that these people continue to *remain* in a local church without truly knowing Christ. They may have repented in the past, coming to the point of believing that Jesus is God and Savior. However, that repentance did not *lead* them to salvation. They got distracted by this or that, and they did not enter into a viable, living relationship with Him, so if one were to point out that the particular local church they attend is fraught with

---

[46] Charles C. Ryrie, *So Great Salvation* (Chicago: Moody Publishers 1997), 86

error, they would generally deny it, and possibly even become incensed by the charge.

The Emergent Church does not teach true salvation and it downplays the need for it. (Seventh Day Adventism does not teach authentic salvation either, because it adds requirements to God's free gift.) The Emergent Church is more concerned with making people feel good through entertainment, than presenting the truth of the Gospel of Jesus Christ. It is more concerned with *quantity*, than *quality*.

The Truth of the Emergent Church

In attending an Emergent Church, you will not hear the fact that all have sinned and are in need of a Savior. You will not attend an Emergent Church that espouses only *one* way of salvation. You may hear that life can be better for you, that you are not that bad off, and that God wants you to be happy. Have your best life now, and much more!

The truth of the matter is that this life will never get better, and it will end. We are all as bad off as we can possibly get because we are without Christ. God does not want us merely happy. God wants our worship and wants us to receive His eternal salvation, which will provide us with *joy,* something far different from happiness. By striving for happiness, we are focused on meeting our own needs. To worship God means submitting ourselves to Him, in order that His purposes will be fulfilled in and through us. This can only be accomplished by individuals who are authentic Christians, those who belong to the *invisible* Church.

The Emergent Church is likely the greatest threat to Christianity this century has known, yet as Christ has said, the gates of hell will not prevail against the Church that He builds. With all of the many avenues involved in the Emergent Church, like Contemplative Prayer, Breath Prayers, use of labyrinths, rosary beads, aspects of Buddhism, mysticism and other forms of New Age mysticism, people who attend church, and even *appear* to be authentic Christians, are in serious danger of falling away from the Truth. Had they gone from realizing the truth to embracing it by receiving His salvation, they would be *protected* from falling away from it. However, because they have *never* fully embraced the Truth, which *would* have led them into a salvific, vital, and living relationship with Jesus Christ, the danger of falling away is ever-present.

That is the Emergent Church. It is a belief system, which offers no absolute truth at all, but mixes *some* truth with error. The Emergent Church is predicated upon beliefs that, at their very heart, stand against God and the Truth that He has revealed in and through Jesus Christ.

Doctrines of Devils
This is the tragedy of living now, as we close in on the beginning of the Tribulation period. Those who believe that the Emergent Church is merely another method of attaining closeness with God will be shocked to learn that they have embraced doctrines of devils. In their search for God, they will have completely left *Him* behind, so intent are they on finding and embracing something that makes them *feel* close to God, while the fact remains that what they hear simply scratches their itchy ears.

The PreTrib Rapture position does *not* scratch itchy ears, nor does it replace God for some other line of thinking that is nothing more than idolatry. The PreTrib Rapture has nothing to do with the falling away that Paul speaks of, because it does not in any way, shape, or form, impinge either directly or indirectly on salvation.

Those who believe that when the Holy Spirit seals believers, that seal is not good enough, strong enough, or eternal in nature, also believe that anything, which can create doubt in someone, is capable of causing them to lose their salvation. They do not believe in eternal security because they think it promotes easy-believism. Since when is the truth of the Gospel, subject to the whims of man, and his propensity to overindulge, or misunderstand?

Unfortunately, I believe these individuals are wrong regarding an authentic Christian's ability to lose salvation. They are also wrong, in my opinion, on the nature of the PreTrib Rapture position. What is needed today is for authentic Christians to be vigilant. We must be vigilant for those who are not only in the visible Church, but also outside the invisible Church. They are in danger of falling away because they are not authentic Christians. We need to be aware of the possibility that some within our local assembly do not really know Christ and therefore will continue to look to other systems, movements, and isms when things get tough for them.

Of course, it behooves us to have correct views about doctrines like salvation. Either all of salvation is God's plan, accomplished by His strength, which we receive through faith, or it is received in faith, and continued with works by each believer.

Salvation begins with a repentance that sees the truth of Jesus Christ. This repentance can lead to a saving faith. If it does, it culminates in the reality of His presence in our lives, and the sealing of the Holy Spirit. To believe authentic Christians can lose salvation is a much greater deception than anything that is connected to Eschatology.

Resources:

- *A Time of Departing* by Ray Yungen
- *Faith Undone* by Roger Oakland
- http://www.lighthousetrailsresearch.com/

Chapter 6

Contemplative Prayer

JESUS (EXHALE)...JESUS (EXHALE)
JESUS (EXHALE)...JESUS (EXHALE)
JESUS (EXHALE)...JESUS (EXHALE)

©2010 F. DERUVO

P rayer is always important. The authentic Christian cannot survive without it, though many apparently believe they can. As far as prayer is concerned, two things are important:

1. *The content of your praying*
2. *To Whom the prayer is directed*

Contemplative Prayer (also sometimes referred to as Contemplative Spirituality), is a type of praying that is best defined as mystical. Quoting from the Lighthouse Trails Research Project, we learn that *"a belief system that uses ancient mystical practices to induce altered states of consciousness (the silence) and is often wrapped in Christian terminology; the premise of contemplative spirituality is pantheistic (God is all) and panentheistic (God is in all)."*[47]

Exactly what is Contemplative Prayer then, under this system described above? Again, from Lighthouse Trails, *"The purpose of contemplative prayer is to enter an altered state of consciousness in order to find one's true self, thus finding God. This true self relates to the belief that man is basically good. Proponents of contemplative prayer teach that all human beings have a divine center and that all, not just born again believers, should practice contemplative prayer."*[48]

Just how does contemplative prayer result in an altered state of consciousness? With respect to the practice of Contemplative Prayer, proponents of this practice speak of using a method they term 'breath prayers.' This is the method whereby one word or short phrase is uttered as the person exhales. For instance, repeating the word "Jesus," while exhaling over time literally empties the mind.

Many practitioners of breath prayers, or contemplative praying, believe that they have become 'still' before the Lord, which places them in the mindset to be able to 'hear' the Lord speak to them. In short, they have entered an altered state of consciousness.

This emptying of the mind, through repetition of words or phrases, achieves a consciousness shift. This consciousness shift results in the brain (or parts of the brain), no longer being controlled by the practitioner. Ray Yungen, in his book *A Time of Departing*, as well as other authors, explains that by continuing to repeat words or phrases,

---

[47] http://www.lighthousetrailsresearch.com/cp.htm
[48] Ibid

not only is the mind emptied, but what literally occurs is an absence of thought. This absence of thought actually allows the enemy to fill that emptiness with *his* thoughts and concepts, which are of course, opposed to God. This type of mysticism dates back for centuries and much of Christendom has been infiltrated by these ancient techniques, which few see difficulty in using.

Trick or Treat

Rich Warren, Richard Foster and numerous other postmodern luminaries, promote this type of prayer in the many books and articles they have written. *"Is Rick Warren promoting contemplative spirituality (i.e., spiritual formation)? We believe the answer to that is a wholehearted "yes." The first clue came many years ago in Warren's first book, The Purpose Driven Church, where he said that the Spiritual Formation movement had a "vital message for the church," and has "given the body of Christ a wakeup call" (p. 127). Since then, a repeated promotion of contemplative prayer has taken place through Rick Warren's ministries."*[49]

Sadly, what is often seen as something beneficial for the individual Christian, and therefore the Church, is often nothing more than New Age mysticism clothed in Christian garb. It is fast becoming the norm for many churches today.

Lance Witt, a pastor at Rick Warren's church, points to Thomas Merton as someone to look up to and emulate with respect to the practice of contemplative praying. Witt believes that utilizing breath prayers (contemplative prayer), allows our minds to literally change frequencies.

This then, allows us to supposedly 'hear' the Father, as He speaks to us. *"This 'changing frequencies' is contemplative language and means going into an Alpha state of mind (an altered state of consciousness) in order*

---

[49] http://www.lighthousetrailsresearch.com/newsletter033006.htm#article2

to stop distractions. It's like putting the mind in neutral. Contemplatives believe this is how they can hear the voice of God."[50]

Are We Really Supposed to Empty Our Minds?

It is often taught that God wants us to empty our minds and the most commonly used portion of Scripture is Psalm 46:10, which states *"Be still, and know that I am God: I will be exalted among the heathen, I will be exalted in the earth."*

The problem of course, is that in this particular Psalm, God is not saying anything about emptying our minds. He is stating that we should be still before Him, and *watch* Him work. It is no different from a parent telling a rambunctious child to "sit still." In that case, it would be completely *incorrect* to argue that the parent is telling the child to empty his or her mind. The child is simply being told to *cease from their activity*, or to *calm down.*

Contemplative Prayer (or breath prayers) is nothing more than modern day mysticism, brought to the present from the ancient past. The focus of contemplative praying is on the individual who is praying.

God speaks to us through His written Word, but too many today are going beyond it, thinking that if they can just hear what God has to say to them directly, they will be better off. This view not only circumvents His written Word, but also creates the false notion that His written Word is not as important as what He might actually be willing to verbalize to us. It also assumes that He is still *speaking* today, in dreams, visions, and other means, and adding new insights into His written Word.

The authentic Christian, who wants to know God's Word, must be devoted to studying His written Word. It is there, that God's will is revealed. There is so much in His written Word, which we are

---

[50] http://www.lighthousetrailsresearch.com/newsletter033006.htm#article2

109

responsible to know and put into practice. That it should occupy us until either we are taken to Him, or He returns. Instead, we use highly dubious practices that draw on mysticism to gain closeness with God. The emphasis is without question, on us.

People always want *more* where God is concerned, yet often these same individuals do not read and obey the written revelation of His will. They go beyond it, seeking to know Him through what He may choose to say to us. What He has chosen to say to us is written down for us. It eliminates the guessing and it shows the way.

Chapter 7

Spiritual Formation

Celebration

LET'S ALL CATCH THE RHYTHM OF
WORSHIP AND PARTY HEARTY!

©2010 F. DERUVO

Spiritual Formation is akin to Contemplative Prayer, in that the latter is really part of the former. It is a spiritual discipline, whereby those who practice it are believed to become closer to God. Willow Creek Association, known for its emphasis on Spiritual Formation says this, "*The Practice offers Saturday morning meetings which provide a **rhythm of worship**, teaching on a particular spiritual* *discipline and time to experience or 'practice' that discipline. This practice time allows participants to get a fuller understanding of how to incorporate the discipline in their daily lives,"*[51] (Emphasis added).

What other things are said to provide a rhythm for our life? The biggest is Transcendental Meditation, which is said to help us become one with the universe and ourselves. Tai Chi, another discipline is also said to help us center ourselves. There are a number of oriental and eastern mystical practices, which boast of their ability to help individuals achieve oneness, or a semblance of spiritual calm, and centering.

What has become more commonplace within Christendom today is the melding of these ancient mystical arts with Christianity, as if that could really occur. Many people believe that it somehow creates a more dynamic relationship with our Creator.

What all of this can and often *does* lead to is reliance upon these disciplines, along with any experience stemming from them. It is not long before the disciplines *themselves* become the final authority. This moves God's written Word to the back burner, or off the stove altogether. The final arbiter for what is correct is how the person *feels* inside. In essence, the person becomes the final authority. Gone is the objective truth of God's Word, replaced with a practice that relies on mysticism and how one feels about it.

In the final analysis, Spiritual Formation *includes* the discipline of Contemplative Prayer, as one aspect of the overall discipline.

---

[51] http://www.lighthousetrailsresearch.com/spiritualformation.htm

Chapter 8

Good Ol' Ecumenism

ECUMENISM TAKES PARTS FROM ALL TO MAKE ONE
(WE ARE ALL PART OF THE DIVINE)

The Ecumenical Movement has been around for decades. Its main goal is to unify and unite all religions, so that all can work toward the overarching goal of creating a better society than the one that currently exists now. Ultimately, what is emphasized is a greater cooperation among adherents of all religions. It is understood that in order to accomplish this, *doctrine* or *dogma* must be set aside in favor of deferring to the other person.

Dogmatism is not only *not* encouraged, but frowned upon. After all, how can people unite in one cause if some believe that Jesus *is* God, while others have a difficult time believing that He actually existed? It should become obvious that the modern ecumenical movement is nothing more than the Tower of Babel revisited (cf. Genesis 11), or today's version of Babylon.

Attempting Oneness

In the course of attempting to build this particular tower, the Bible tells us *"the whole earth was of one language, and of one speech. And it came to pass, as they journeyed from the east, that they found a plain in the land of Shinar; and they dwelt there. And they said one to another, Go to, let us make brick, and burn them thoroughly. And they had brick for stone, and slime had they for morter. And they said, Go to, let us build us a city and a tower, whose top may reach unto heaven; and let us make us a name, lest we be scattered abroad upon the face of the whole earth,"* (Genesis 11:1-4 KJV).

In the above narrative, people came together for one purpose. Their purpose included building a tower, which reached to heaven. They were interested in making a *name* for themselves. They wanted their name and reputation to precede them and to stand for generations.

Of course, God saw what was happening, and decided to interrupt their plans. He did this, as we are told in the following verses, by confusing their languages and cultures. From that point on, people went their own way, grouping together based on the languages they spoke. These groups then dispersed to other areas.

What has been occurring within the Ecumenical Movement is the desire to once again, become one in purpose. While the goal is not necessarily to build a physical tower that reaches to the heavens, it is clear that the people involved in this movement want to make a name. There is no way for the authentic Christian to be involved in this movement, without compromising the very tenets of Orthodox Christianity, yet this is what is being done and this is what is expected of those who become part of this movement.

Attempting Oneness in 2010

How is it possible for people of all different faiths to come together under one religious banner, and be expected to set aside beliefs that may conflict with other individuals also involved? It is only possible if people see their convictions as *secondary*. They can only set aside the Orthodox Christian tenets, if they do not see them as important as working together. If they do not see them as important, then the question of their eternal salvation comes into question.

Please do not misunderstand. It is necessary and good for people to work together, and they will likely find themselves working with other individuals of other faiths. However, when the *stated goal* is to *unify* all people of various faiths and beliefs under one umbrella, nothing good can come of that.

This has been Satan's goal from the beginning, to pull people away from God, and make them believe that specific beliefs or doctrines do not matter. What matters is the oneness of all people, the oneness of societal norms. As people work together for the common good, everything becomes clearly watered down, and nothing stands out as truth, because all of it becomes truth.

Authentic Christians cannot be part of an organization that demands allegiance to generalized religious goals. In essence, the authentic Christian is being asked to repudiate what he/she strongly believes. To do so, is to fall away from the faith by replacing it with something far less worthy.

Don't Worry, Be Unified

Like ecumenism, which seeks to unify those within various religious denominations, there is a movement afoot within society (bypassing established religion), to unify people. The thrust of the unity movement is for people to become one in purpose.

As discussed, the Tower of Babel was man's attempt to become unified under one leader, Nimrod. Ultimately, national leaders such as Nimrod, Hitler, Mussolini and religious leaders like David Koresh, Jim Jones, Sun Yung Moon and many others all have one thing in common; they are very charismatic and they know how to win people to their side of the aisle.

However, society contains many people who prefer to go with the status quo. They do not necessarily want to have to be the one to make the decisions, nor do they really even want to be part of the group that makes those decisions. Often though, these same people tend to cry the loudest when they feel their needs are not being met. Nonetheless, these individuals are often susceptible to frauds, cults and the like, all because, rather than dealing with issues themselves, and possibly feeling left out, they will go with the flow to ensure their involvement.

If we take the time to step back, and begin to see the world as one large community, it is not long before we will also begin to recognize the signs and movements that are attempting to become established with one purpose. Throughout history, man has attempted one way or another to lift himself to the highest level, believing that if he tries hard enough, he will surpass even God (or the Christ Consciousness, or something else entirely).

Satan began this effort and passed the desire along to humanity. Once our first parents – Adam and Eve – adopted it for themselves, it became the modus operandi for humanity in general. Every so often, someone claws his way to the top of the human heap, declaring this or that, promising humanity (or their region of the world), great things they will receive from him. Often, a mob mentality can take hold and people play follow the leader, just like we did as children. Of course, the stakes are infinitely higher than the game we once played.

Whether through a religious venue, or a humanistic one, Satan's plans have really not changed all that much since Creation. He continues his attempts to thwart God's plans by turning man from God, inward.

Ultimately, while his schemes will ensnare many, God has the victory. God is the One who will be standing in the end, when all the dust clears. He will be glorified and all will bow the knee to the only wise and deserving God, our Father.

Chapter 9

Bringing in the Kingdom

D ominion Theology (consisting of Kingdom Now and Christian Reconstructionism), seeks to usher in God's eternal kingdom by working for it now. Proponents of this theology believe that God is waiting for things to improve in society until such a point where He will be able to return. Apparently, this involves more and more people becoming Christians. As more become Christians, God has more to work through, to achieve His goals for humanity and this planet.

The problem with this view is that it makes God subservient to humanity. There He sits, presumably on His throne, waiting patiently until those of the earthy slowly, but steadily turns to Him. Once the perfect time is reached (known only to God), He will then be able to physically return to earth, and set up His Kingdom.

Over the years, there have been several versions of this type of theology, which has motivated those within Christendom. Jerry Falwell's political organization, The Moral Majority, is a type of Dominism, since it is believed that through the political process, laws would be enacted, which will mold society for the better.

Often, but not always, Reformed and/or Covenant Theologians adopt Dominion Theology, because many of them reject a literal interpretation of Eschatology, preferring instead to view things allegorically. This means that Jesus reigns now, not at some later point from David's actual throne in Jerusalem, and only for a mere 1,000 years.

Reformed theologians also often subscribe to the view that the Tribulation has already occurred, with Nero (or somebody else) as the Antichrist. The Antichrist is not so much a person, but a spirit, or demeanor, which guides many individuals (Hitler, etc.), to perpetrate terrible horrors on humanity, or one particular group within humanity.

All of these views tend to place God in the waiting area. As His followers, we work hard here in this life, to bring His goals to fruition. Once the necessary level is reached, He will then be able to come back and set up His kingdom, for all of eternity.

Unfortunately, this view is very much like the view that Muslims hold. They await the final Mahdi, the Imam, who will be the savior of the world. It is said that he is waiting in the wings, able to reveal himself only at the proper time. No one knows when that proper time will arrive.

Interestingly enough, many rank and file Islamists believe that as they work hard to turn this entire world into one governed by Allah, through the laws of Islam being established worldwide, the final Mahdi will be able to reveal himself to all of humanity.

Christ Said it Would Get Bad

What many people seem unaware of, or simply refuse to believe, is that Christ Himself talked about the state of this world, and what it would come to, prior to His Second Coming. Instead, people want to believe that we can make this a better place and eventually solve all the problems we face, because of how God made us. This may have been true prior to the fall, but it certainly does not exist now and there is no way that given the state of affairs, and the record of Scripture, anyone should expect to see the world improve.

The fact remains that the world is getting worse and Christ promised that it would get much worse, before He returns. All one has to do is read the Olivet Discourse previously discussed to know that this is the case. This idea that the world is progressively worsening flies in the face of those who believe the opposite and that man can somehow create a better society through sheer willpower and obedience.

Of course (and before being misunderstood), what I am *not* saying is that Christians should ignore social issues. Neither should we pretend that there is no point in recycling, or doing our part to save what we can save. We are all stewards of this earth and its resources should be used *wisely*.

When we see people who are in less fortunate situations than we are, we should do what we can to ease their stress, by helping them in whatever way we can. This does not mean though, that by doing this, we are giving assent to the Dominion Now theology. Many so-called Christians go far overboard, believing that by simply fixing the socials ills in the world, people will become closer to the God of the Bible. In fact, people like Tony Campolo and others argue that for those who are involved in taking care of people's needs, and minimizing suffering, they are in fact, already in relationship with Christ, whether they are Islamic, Buddhist, or affiliated with no religion.

This mentality however, minimizes actual salvation to the extent that it becomes secondary. In the most extreme cases, authentic salvation provided by Jesus Christ is not even on the table. The more important thing is to see to it that social needs are met for those who suffer.

Let us be unequivocally clear with reference to this subject. Every authentic Christian must not only preach the Gospel, but also take care of the needs of others, as they are able. However, the preaching of the Gospel is always first, because no one knows when another is going to die.

Before Christ fed the multitudes on several occasions, He always presented the truth of the Gospel first. He realized of course, that physical needs were important, but they pale in comparison to the spiritual needs that all people have inside them. If all professing Christians do is meet the physical needs of others, without providing the Gospel message verbally, the only thing that has been accomplished is that a physical need has been met. Long after that physical need is met, and may need to be met again, the spiritual need was never addressed.

There has to be a balance, but when push comes to shove, the Gospel should never be pushed off the table. It should be presented accurately, passionately and without fail. To do any less is to live in disobedience to the Great Commission.

Chapter 10

They're Out of this World

THEY COME IN PEACE, PREDICTING APOCALYPTIC ANNIHILATION...

...UNLESS WE HEED THEIR WISDOM, WE WILL SELF-DESTRUCT!

THEY ARE ELOHIM, MAKERS OF ALL LIFE ON PLANET EARTH!

THEY ARE GOD!

(ACTUALLY, THEY ARE PROBABLY DEMONS!)

(NOTE TAIL!)

©2010 F. DERUVO

Somewhere, out there, are aliens, or extraterrestrials, if you will. These space beings have apparently come to earth many times, for many purposes, but their overarching purpose seems to be to warn humanity of impending doom.

It does not matter who you read from the field of UFOology. Authors like Barbara Marciniak and others are sending up warnings. These dire predictions spell out a future of an apocalyptic nature. This is fascinating of course, when one stops to consider the fact that there are groups of people who espouse Dominion Theology, believing that we can work it out, just as the Beatles sang in 1963. So if we have two groups of people voicing opposing opinions, whom do you believe?

Approach of the Apocalypse

Yes, we are approaching an apocalypse, but one that was plainly set by God, if we are to take Scripture seriously. The final battle between puny humankind and omnipotent God is too sad to be funny, yet that is what humanity is heading for, and God in Christ is waiting to address it, when He returns physically to the earth at some yet, future, undisclosed time.

On one hand, the "aliens" are telling us that we are headed for disaster, unless we change our ways. On the other hand, the Dominion Theology people are telling us that as we work together, preaching the Gospel, and seeing more and more people being converted to Christianity, God will return.

Both of these scenarios tell only part of the story, and because of that, they are both essentially useless. Aliens (most probably demons in disguise), are teaching the world that the apocalypse is most certainly in the future and without their help, there is no detour. It must be asked what these aliens/demons hope to gain from their endeavor?

Since they are telling part of the truth, they obviously want to be looked at as saviors; role models that people of this world can look up to, and strive to become like, as we give ear to their wisdom and solutions.

As authors like Chuck Missler and others have pointed out though, it seems strange that these aliens promise that they can help us, yet all of their messages received by the aforementioned Marciniak and others, deal with *religion*. You would think that they might at least drop a hint about how to cure cancer, or eliminate AIDS, or the common cold forever. They do not do this, instead speaking of a person who will come to save all of humanity. Interesting.

Some of these alien messages also have pointed to a cataclysmic event they call the "great evacuation." This particular event is slated to occur because there are those on this planet who keep the rest from evolving to the next level, apparently. It is interesting to read their description of something that sounds very much like the Rapture. They say that "in the twinkling of an eye," upwards of 20 million people or more will be removed from this planet, taken to space ships above the earth's atmosphere. From there, they will be taken to the "mother ship," then to another "plane." Those who remain should not weep for them because apparently, these 20 million will go to a "happy place," or "home" to see loved ones and family.

You can read more about all of this in Chuck Missler's (with Mark Eastman) book *Alien Encounters*. It retails for $9.95 and can be ordered from Missler's site, www.khouse.org.

Chapter 11

Mysticism Breaks Wind

S adly, numerous forms of mysticism have worked their way into the visible Church. They all seem to emanate from within the Emergent Church. However, prior to the realization that a postmodern movement to be named the Emergent Church existed within Christendom, various forms of ethereal thought and mysticism has held sway. In many ways then, these various forms of mysticism have merely paved the way for the surfacing of the Emergent Church, also known as the Postmodern Church.

Way back in the 1970s, the Charismatic movement took hold of many churches throughout the world. To my chagrin, I came to be part of this. At that time, I was not well versed in the Bible, and tended to seek God through my emotions. This fit well within the Charismatic movement because (unfortunately), the movement in many ways thrived on emotion. I am sure many will disagree with this assessment; nonetheless, this is what seemed prominent to me at the time.

Beginnings of Tongues

The Charismatic movement dates back to Father Dennis Bennett, an Episcopalian priest, who in the early 1960s published his book *Nine O'clock in the Morning*. The book, among other things, described what he termed the *outpouring of the Holy Spirit*. He made a distinction between the baptism of the Holy Spirit, which occurs at the moment of salvation, and the *empowering*, which he believed occurred at a later date, just as the birth of the authentic Church experienced in Acts 2.

The movement gained popularity through Bennett's book and the conferences, which followed, where he ministered to individuals who desired what Bennett himself had experienced. The main highlights of the Charismatic movement included:

- *Speaking in tongues*
- *Healings*
- *Prophecies*
- *The giving of a 'word of knowledge'*
- *Overcoming demonic spirits*
- *A variety of other sign gifts*

What I personally came to realize about the Charismatic movement is that I found myself seeking after experiences. With such an emphasis on the experiential nature of the supernatural, it is reasonable to conclude that my own emphasis was also the experience of many. The experiential nature of the Charismatic Movement was difficult to avoid.

I do not remember one meeting I attended that did not emphasize the spectacular, or supernatural. This emphasis, that really created unrealistic expectations from people, became the norm. Most meetings I attended included people who gave *words of knowledge*. These words of knowledge were often viewed as God speaking in the present to those gathered to hear Him.

Over time, I began to question the validity of these "special" words of knowledge, because most were very general in nature, or simply a reiteration of Scripture. Why do I need to go to a meeting to hear someone speak Scripture as a word of knowledge, when I could read the same Scripture (more precisely), directly out of the Bible? Isn't God's Word living and active, whether it is read or spoken?

May I Have a Word *for* You?
The other thing I began to notice is that people would go to other people with a 'word' for them. They would share this word, which they believed was directly from God. I questioned this practice, because I wondered why God Himself would not impress upon a specific individual what He wanted them to know. Why did He use one person to tell another? It was not as if the person who was being told was out of fellowship either.

Of course, some defended this practice, referring to examples from both the Old and New Testaments. However, there are a number of reasons I believe these words were given then. First, in the Old Testament, the Holy Spirit never took up permanent residence within any of those saints. He would often come upon them when they were appointed for a specific purpose, and then leave them when their job was complete.

In the New Testament, we see that after the Church was born, it went through a period where it became established. This process lasted through the time of the last apostle, and then history shows us that the sign-gifts went away.

Nonetheless, people still disagree with this, believing that since God is the same yesterday, today and forever, these gifts once established would exist for all time. There are numerous arguments that rebut this position, which have already been thoroughly presented in other works.

It's All About the Inner Experience

My point here is that because of the Charismatic movement and other movements that followed like, Latter Rain, Holy Laughter and the like, the visible Church began to look more toward the inner *experience* of being a Christian, rather than simply submitting our will for His. The focus had become "what can I experience from my union with Christ" instead of "what can I submit to Him today that He might work in and through me for His glory?"

This type of thinking – where the emphasis turns inward – plays out by an increased focus on one's self. How can one possibly grow in Christ, if our focus is on ourselves? This may be completely my fault; however, I did not see much that taught me (or others) anything different.

There is one thing I did learn through my association with the Charismatic movement and it is something that I believe to be biblical, viable, and necessary for growth in Christ. I learned how to *praise* Him, even in circumstances that created fear and/or doubt within me. I continue that practice to this day.

Another movement that became known within Christendom was called the Toronto Blessing, but also became known as Holy Laughter. Having started in a Toronto church that met at an airport, the emphasis was on *laughter* during the service. It was believed (and still is by many) that during services, the Holy Spirit would pour out His blessing, which often exhibited itself in uncontrollable laughter throughout the congregation, or other visible signs. Individuals would find themselves laughing hysterically, sliding off chairs, or falling to the ground, until the entire assembly was row after row of laughing people.

Bellying Up to the Bar

Eventually, evangelist Rodney Howard-Browne became the go-to guy here, and even became known as "God's bartender." During his meetings, people would laugh and laugh, oh and did I say, laugh? Oh, it was just hilarious. As one can imagine, little to no preaching was done during these services. Howard-Browne merely presented himself and often, the laughter began. Sometimes, instead of laughter, animal noises were emitted by people in attendance, such as the roaring of a lion, or the clucking of a chicken. These are believed by adherents to be the various manifestations of the Holy Spirit in power.

What one possibly gains by laughing hysterically during what is supposed to be a worship service, is only a guess. This laughter is said to be the movement of the Holy Spirit, bringing Christians into a deeper relationship with God. But how? What is the result of laughing your brains out? Does a person come away with more knowledge of Scripture that can be applied to one's life? Do people press on toward holiness before God? It would appear not. It would appear that this is merely another attempt by the enemy of our souls to wreak havoc in the Christian's life by catering to the demands of emotion.

Even though this movement peaked out in the mid-1990s, Howard-Browne and other leaders within this movement are still around. Since the establishment of the Charismatic movement in the United States in the 1960s, except for a period of a few years here and there, it has really been a constant stream of one form of mysticism after another that has embraced and/or found its way into the visible Church.

It is fairly easy to see how the enemy has worked to establish a pattern within Christendom that sets people up for change through experience. The Emergent Church is simply another form of Christianity that emphasizes *experience*, and the Emergent Church seeks not to disappoint either. While much of what occurs within the Emergent Church is designed to be more cerebral in nature (asking questions, and discussing possibilities), there are aspects of it, as has been previously shown, which cater to the experiential side of humanity.

Whether it is a labyrinth, where practitioners walk a labyrinth path, while reciting certain words or phrases, or whether they repeat breath prayers while fondling Rosary beads, the emphasis is on experiencing more of Christ. These systems accomplish this it is said, by allowing the practitioner to empty his or her mind. Once empty, God can then speak, revealing a new level of understanding for the individual, which promotes a deeper, more effective walk as a Christian.

The problem of course, is that while there is a real experiential side to Christianity, to strive after that is not what we are commissioned to do. What we are called to do is submit ourselves to Him, in order that we might become vessels for Him to use, to bring the lost to Him for salvation. It is in this that He is glorified.

For the Christian who believes (as I once did), that the pursuit of Christ involves determining what I can get out of it, how I can feel because of my established union with Him, and what my union with Him does for me in the here and now, we wind up circumventing God's purposes and plans for us. It is obvious from Scripture that true Christians will experience joy, which bubbles up from within, to overflowing. Why is that joy there? It is there only as we are united in purpose with Him and that purpose is to fulfill His will for us. His will does not mean that we concentrate on what we can gain from Him as we live this life now. His will means that we concentrate on what we need to get rid of by submitting to Him, in order that He will be able to live His will out in and through us.

The focus is never us. The focus is always Him and the lost of this world. The mystical elements, which found their way into the visible Church, broke down barriers. They established themselves, and created an atmosphere, in which chasing after the *experience* became the norm. Since people grow tired of the same experience, the initial experience needs to be replaced with something else, something new. This is what has occurred and what continues to occur.

The Emergent Church and everything associated with it, is simply the more mature brother of mysticism, which began the last century with the Charismatic movement. Through the Emergent Church, people's barriers are broken down, and they become open to that which they believe will give them something.

What is needed is not some*thing*. What is needed is Christ alone. Our union with Him should be enough, but for far too many people today, it is not. We think we need more. We think we need the latest experience to deepen our relationship with God. We do not. We need less of ourselves, which ultimately provides more room for God to work.

Never Enough
In the Garden of Eden, Adam and Eve lived in a perfect environment. It was sinless. Adam and Eve walked with God, speaking with Him face to face. There was no pain, there was no sickness, there was no want and there was certainly no death. Yet, this was not even good enough *then*, in spite of the perfection of the environment and the absence of sin, pain and death.

In today's world, we continue to make the same mistake that Adam and Eve made; deciding that the next experience, or greater worldly knowledge will provide what we are missing, or give us greater insight and more maturity. This mysticism within the visible Church has been drawing people away from the true faith. Paul refers to this epidemic when he states that in the End Times, there will be a great falling away.

What else would prepare the world for a one-world government? What else will make everyone believe they must unite as one in order to survive? What else would come to the fore, which will cause people to believe that all they need is one man who will lead the world into an eternal time of peace? The belief in the PreTrib Rapture does not do this, folks. It is the call of *mysticism* that does this, and whether this mysticism is found within the visible Church, or within the New Age movement outside of the visible Church, it all leads to the same error; the belief that all roads lead to God and Christ is merely one of those ways. When people get to that point, they have fallen away from the true faith. They have replaced the One True God, with that of an idol.

Chapter 12

Sensitivity Training Needed

WHAT? ALL I SAID WAS THAT YOU REMIND ME OF THE CAT IN THE HAT!

©2010 F. DERUVO

One of the first books I published is called *The Anti-Supernatural Bias of Ex-Christians.* People seem to enjoy it, unless they are atheists or ex-Christians (a misnomer, by the way). These folks are convinced that God does not at all exist. They do not like it when people question their previous alleged commitment to Jesus, or whether or not they actually were in fact, Christians. It is hurtful to them and even judgmental, they say. Who is anyone to question whether they were in fact, Christians? They say they were and that should be good enough. Never mind that now, some deny that Jesus ever existed, while others deny that God exists (assuming for the sake of argument that Jesus is not God).

The problem is me, they say. I am not sensitive enough to the harm my words might cause to others living on this planet. I should not be so dogmatic because it is this very dogmatism that destroys, they say. In fact, I should take sensitivity training so that I can learn to say things without hurting others.

What Say You?
However, if we consider Jesus (who talked about hell more than any other subject by the way), we see in Him a Person who loved people. He loved them so much, that He was willing to die for them. He loved them so much that He was willing to go out on a limb and say that He and He alone was the only way to God (cf. John 14:6). Now, either He was a liar, or the words He used had very different definitions from these words today.

It is the height of hypocrisy and arrogance to assume that Jesus is the only way to God, to believe that salvation only comes through Jesus Christ and Him alone. This is what the world tells Christians. Make no mistake about it; many Christians continue to lay down their lives in torture and death throughout the world over this one issue.

The diabolical way in which people *hate* Christians says a good deal about Jesus and Satan. These satanically inspired attitudes and ideas about Christians stem from Satan's own hatred of God, and therefore *us*, the crown of God's creation.

Satan wants nothing more than to see every one of the individuals on this planet die without ever having received Christ's salvation. He wants them to go into eternity completely blind to the fact that there *is* a salvation, and that it is *one* salvation, only found in Jesus Christ, no ifs, ands or buts.

Satan has convinced this world (his temporary kingdom), that what Christians preach is a complete lie. He has convinced his followers that they not only do *not* need God in Christ, but there is a huge question about whether or not Jesus actually existed at all!

Proud of Being an "Ex"

Speak to someone who says – with pride – that he or she is an "ex-Christian." You will find among these individuals, people who were pastors, religious teachers, choir members, church members, Sunday school teachers and more. They will tell you all the things they did in God's Name. They will boast of speaking in tongues, praying for people to be healed (and they were!), attending church regularly, giving a tenth of their income, reading their Bible, praying, going door-to-door witnessing and a plethora of other things that they firmly believe qualifies them as Christians.

However, the one thing they lacked was a vital, living relationship with Jesus Christ. They *never* had that. This spiritual transaction is only the beginning of a lifelong relationship with Jesus, which continues to the point of our death and into eternity. Being "born again," as Christ explained to Nicodemus in John 3, is *supernatural*. It originates in the supernatural and completes itself in the supernatural.

No other religion or religious system exists, which has as its leader, an Individual who was willing to die, and *did* die so that many might receive salvation. Jesus Christ paid the price for the sins of humanity. All who choose to believe Him can have that salvation.

Somewhere, in the case of the ex-Christian, something went wrong. They "know" they were Christians, yet everything in the Bible speaks against that fact. In spite of this, they will not listen, and they are not alone. Most will not listen. Most become angry when someone attempts to explain the message of the cross of Christ. Satan inspires their anger. This is not to say that those individuals are possessed (though some certainly could be). It is to say that this anger probably takes many of these people by complete surprise, yet they go with it. They *choose* to allow that anger to speak for them, and it does. They find this excuse or that excuse for rejecting Christ, and in the end, what they have done is committed spiritual suicide.

In a world that is hurtling toward eternity, with hundreds (if not thousands), of souls entering in through the door of their deaths, they must be told that Jesus is the only way. Sensitivity training? While Christians are supposed to be as wise as serpents and as gentle as doves, the fact remains that people must be told that Satan is waging a battle for their soul. They must be told that they are sinners and yet, there is a way out for them. Christ Himself provided the way.

Rejecting His Love
Many will reject this wonderful message of love. We can convince no one of the truth of Scripture. Still, our job is to tell them, with love, with firmness and with an absolute desire to see each person come to a saving knowledge of salvation, through the Person of Jesus Christ, even if it means the laying down of our life in some mission field.

If we really love people, that is sensitivity training enough. The love of God prompted Him to be born of a virgin, live a life of full humanity (yet never divorced from His deity), die a brutally painful and bloody death on the cross, only to rise again because death could not hold Him. This raised life is what offers salvation to all. Only those who believe Christ to be who He says He is, have any chance of receiving His salvation.

If someone was trying to get back into a burning house to save something of importance to him or her, you do not try to calmly reason with him or her. It may well be that you will need to get in their face about the dangers of what they are trying to do. It may be that you physically block them from going into that house, because entering that inferno means certain death.

Thousands of people filter in and out of our lives daily. Many, if not most, are headed toward an eternity without God. How can we allow that to happen? How can we let them pass by without so much as a word, or a prayer for their salvation?

As Paul would say, "Brothers, this ought not to be." This is fact though that we allow too many to walk right by us hardly even noticing them, much less witnessing to them, or praying for them.

Jesus never lost an opportunity to explain to people the way to God. He never missed a chance to explain the gospel and that He and He alone was the fulfillment of it. Can we do no less?

If sensitivity training means learning to say things that do not offend others, then this is not what the Christian needs. The Christian needs to be trained to be sensitive to God's leading. We need to learn to see people through God's eyes and be ready to explain to them God's love, as witnessed by the supreme sacrifice of Jesus' death and shed blood on the cross and His resurrection three days later. If they never hear, how will they ever be able to decide?

Chapter 13

Green with Gaia

The subtlety of the Going Green movement keeps it from being seen for what it is; a reverse of God's order. In other words, we have the working hypothesis of evolution, which essentially states that all life came from...*nothing*. What evolutionists actually say is that all life came from the right grouping of specific molecules, and at just the right time, life began. There has been no adequate explanation about *how* these things took place, or for that matter, where the original molecules came from which are credited with beginning the entire process. This creates no problem for scientists or adherents of evolution because science is always seen as being *in discovery*. Scientists are allowed to say (with frequency), that it is not now known how life began, but they are confident that they will know...one day. Until then, people should simply be patient.

Not What it Seems

It is interesting how people routinely accept comments like these because they *seem* to make sense. On the other hand, if scientists cannot unequivocally state how life actually began on this planet, then why should I believe anything else science states about the origin of the species or how things developed? When I refuse to take some scientist's word for things, I am seen as narrow, infantile, a believer in fairy tales (God created), naïve and much more. I lack the brainpower and skill to fully understand how far science has allegedly come from its humble beginnings.

This book is not meant to be a treatise against evolution. I mention it because it shows how the world thinks. For much of the world, that life came from non-life is beyond question. We are merely waiting for all of the information to come to the fore. The truth of evolution is a foregone conclusion though, and those who do not get on the bandwagon of evolution, are nothing more than misguided, narrow minded religious clods, keeping society from evolving to the next level. I was not aware that I had that much power, but okay.

Along with the belief in the fairy tale of evolution, comes the growing demand to be "green." This means taking care of our world and not using up its resources. We need to save them for the next generation of people. Never mind that there are plenty of people alive now who could benefit from them. To use these resources unchecked is plainly selfishness at its worst. We need to respect "Gaia," our mother, the earth.

Please do not get me wrong. I am all for using what God has given us wisely, as good stewards of His Creation. However, the problem with both evolution and the Going Green movement is insidious. Because it is insidious, the average person does not quickly discern it.

One of the problems with both Going Green and evolution is that it places humanity on the bottom of the ladder. It turns everything upside down. No longer is the importance of humankind seen, but instead humankind's needs must be secondary, because there are species of trees and animals, which are said to be more important, because of their scarcity.

Drill Somewhere Else!
In the United States, it has become virtually impossible to drill for oil off our own coasts, because of the possibility of nature-endangering oil spills. These have obviously happened in the past, but instead of figuring out a way to get the oil out of the ground by doing as little damage as possible to nature, we outlaw it.

However, we still need oil. Our vehicles run on oil. Many fuel sources for home heating also require oil. So where do we now purchase our oil? From foreign countries. This of course, puts us in the position of relying on the whims of these other governments. When tensions rise between countries (as they always do), natural resources like oil become the thing that increases the tension.

The consumer is still at odds with the major automobile manufacturers. We all want cars that get wonderful mileage. We get tired of paying the constant upwardly mobile climb of the price of gasoline. Why can't cars run on water, or sunlight, we ask. Why have the manufacturers not worked to harness the power of the sun or electricity decades ago?

I remember when the Ford Escape Hybrid came out. The way it works is that energy is created and stored when the brakes are applied. That seems strange to me and I mentioned it to one of the guys at the dealership when I had taken my car in one day. His answer was that there was no other way to build the car so that it would create and store energy.

I am not a scientist, or an inventor, but that answer seemed odd to me. There was *no other way* for an automobile to create and/or store energy, except through the braking system? That made no sense at all. We have solar panels for homes. Why can't we have solar panels for cars? Someone will say that the solar panels for cars would have to be large and very heavy in order to work properly. If that is so, then why can't people continue to work on solar panels until they come up with a design that works very well, yet is extremely small and lightweight?

In all of this though, the main point is that what much of society does is not for man's best interests. What society outlaws is also not for man's best interests. That does not seem to matter though, because it appears as though it is much more important to do something that makes people feel good about saving a tree, or something else.

Years ago, when I was a kid, I recall taking bottles to the grocery store, receiving a few pennies or nickels in exchange. It was nice, because it allowed me to buy some gum, or candy, or even a comic book if I saved enough over time. Eventually, they did away with that, and people simply resorted to throwing away the bottles because they had no other use for them.

We Don't Want Your Bottles, Kid

Then, it wasn't too many years ago that they decided it was important to once again start taking bottles back, however, now they decided to also add a fee onto the purchase of soda, for instance. The stores no longer took bottles back. That became the job of recycling places. You could bring all your cans and bottles to them and receive some change (literally) for all of it. It was often more of a pain than it was worth and only diehard environmentalists would do this.

Now, in most cities, there is a recycling program in place. In my neighborhood, we do not have to separate the recyclables from the rest of the garbage. It all goes in the same bin, and on trash day, the truck comes around, empties the contents of the bin into the back of the truck, then drives to the recycling facility when his truck is full.

At the recycling facility, all the trash is sorted there. Everything and anything that is recyclable is pulled out and readied for recycling. It is a remarkable system really, and one that seems to be down to a science. However, what has really made the recycling industry come of age is the fact that someone figured out how to charge Joe Consumer to take advantage of it. Profits are the motivating factor.

This is the key, at least for the manufacturing industry. Why aren't cars fully electric, taking their power from the sun? Because then Joe Consumer would not need to "fill it up" on a regular basis. The point is that no matter how you slice it, the environmental business is just that – *big business*.

We are told we must conserve, stop wasting, stop cutting down trees, leave the animals alone, and more. However, these are not God's parameters. They are *man's* parameters. God said to subdue the earth (cf. Genesis 2). Man is the crown of God's creation, however to hear environmentalists tell it man's needs should be at the end of the line.

It appears that there are two extremes within the Going Green industry. On the one hand, business interests want to make as much money as possible on recycling. Why should it cost *more* to buy recycled paper, though? On the other hand, radicals within the environmental movement will not be happy until and unless every tree and animal is left alone, very little water is used, no research is completed that could possibly intrude on nature and ultimately, everything in nature is turned upside down, and we are all walking around naked. Instead of humanity being able to *utilize* what God provided for us to use, we have been made to feel that we should go without so that future generations will have something.

Using Does Not Necessarily Mean Wasting

Again, this is not to say that there should be wanton waste. Being a good steward of anything, means to use things as needed but not to simply indulge in wastefulness. There is nothing wrong with cutting down trees, and replacing the ones that have been cut down with young trees, to grow in the place of the harvested trees.

It is impossible for humanity to exist in this world without using the resources that are found on the planet. There obviously needs to be a balance in the way in which resources are utilized by people, but the idea that we must treat everything as if using it is detrimental to our survival is ridiculous.

The plain fact of the matter is that God has decreed that this world will last only so long. At some point in the future, He will destroy it and will create new heavens and a new earth. The new ones He will create will last forever. What we have now, will not.

If allowed, the Going Green movement would place man's needs last, putting all trees, plants and animals before him in importance. This complete reversal is what the enemy wants for us, because it is diametrically opposed to what God has designed. That alone should set off red flags in our heads.

Chapter 14

The Day of the Lord

The timing could not have been more perfect. As I was writing this book, one of my professors from Tyndale Theological Seminary, Dr. David Olander had just published his book on the doctrine of the Rapture. In the book titled, *The Greatness of the Rapture* (published by Tyndale Seminary), he takes great pains to explain the language surrounding numerous areas involving the Rapture of the Church. One of those areas deals with the many passages related to *The*

Day of the Lord. Dr. Olander opens that particular chapter on the Day of the Lord with a quote from Zephaniah 1:14-18.

Day of the Lord's Wrath

Olander notes the absolute importance of the concept of the Day of the Lord, and further points out that "*the doctrine of the day of the Lord is so vital that a thorough understanding is essential for any proper interpretation of eschatology.*"[52] This is precisely where many students of the Bible have erred and it is usually because they see this "day" of the Lord as merely *one* day, as opposed to a period of time.

Olander points out those Scriptures referencing the Day of the Lord have in mind a time of His future, specific wrath. He also points out that the coming Tribulation, of which Christ spoke in the Olivet Discourse is part of this Day of the Lord.

This particular period of wrath, is separate from God's divine wrath, which is seen throughout Scripture, and throughout human history as well. The Day of the Lord, is a period of time, which encompasses the pouring out of His wrath during the Tribulation (which leads into the latter half of the Tribulation; something the Lord referred to as the Great Tribulation, Matthew 24:21). This Day of the Lord also includes His Second Coming.

What makes the *Day of the Lord* so different is the fact that it:

- Comes upon an unbelieving world
- The ensuing destruction is the worst this world will have ever experienced, and will affect the *entire* globe at the same time
- Ends only in the physical return of Jesus Christ

---

[52] Dr. David Olander, *The Greatness of the Rapture* (Ft. Worth: Tyndale Press 2009), 89

None of these things has ever occurred before during any other period of divine wrath. Olander notes many passages, which reflect this doctrinal concept of the Day of the Lord, including (but not limited to):

- Isaiah 13:6; 13:9
- Joel 1:15; 2:1-11; 2:31; 3:14
- Ezekiel 13:5; 30:3
- Amos 5:18, 20
- Obadiah 15
- Zephaniah 1:7, 14-16, 18
- Malachi 4:5
- Acts 2:20
- 1 Corinthians 5:5
- 1 Thessalonians 5:2
- 2 Thessalonians 2:2
- 2 Peter 3:10

Olander also points out that the phrase is used *"several ways in Scripture, but as a general term it views the entire period beginning with the rapture and terminating at the end of the millennium; thus, the day of the Lord involves judgment upon unbelievers but blessing for believers."*[53] We see this in 2 Peter 3:10b-12, where he references the coming eternal state.

Of course, this is exactly what Paul discusses in his letters to the Thessalonians. In fact, Paul clearly delineates the events of this time, leading up to and including the Day of the Lord. While most are familiar with Paul's claim that the Church is not appointed to wrath (cf. 1 Thessalonians 1:10), many disagree over the meaning of the word *wrath*. This is why Olander takes the time to show that the Day of the Lord is referencing a specific period in future history when the entire

---

[53] Dr. David Olander, *The Greatness of the Rapture* (Ft. Worth: Tyndale Press 2009), 93

period will represent God's wrath. While the context deals with our ultimate salvation, it also deals with the Tribulation and the wrath that occurs during that time.

When the apostle Paul gets to chapter five of his first letter to the Thessalonians, he begins to focus in on the events, as they will occur. Let's take a few moments to zero in on that as well. Paul begins chapter five by acknowledging that the believers in Thessalonica did not need to be taught about the times and seasons, since they knew *"that the day of the Lord so cometh as a thief in the night,"* (1 Thessalonians 5:2b KJV).

Coming as a Thief in the Night

The entire unbelieving world will be completely unprepared for the beginning of this future Day of the Lord! It will shock and confound the world. In verse nine, Paul reiterates that the true, invisible Church is not subject to God's wrath. His correction, and His chastisement, yes, but the authentic Christian will *never* experience God's wrath, as this is reserved for *unbelievers*.

From this first letter to the Thessalonians, we learn that the rapture will occur, and then the Day of the Lord will begin. The difficulty here is that many believe the Day of the Lord to be *one* day (His return), with the rapture occurring at the same time, or instantly prior to His return. This is *not* what the Day of the Lord references. As noted, the Day of the Lord includes the Second Coming, but it also includes the time *prior* to His Second Coming, as well as *after* it.

The Day of the Lord begins with the Rapture, prior to the beginning of the Tribulation, and we know from Scripture (Daniel 9), that the Tribulation begins when the Antichrist signs a covenant with Israel, promising them peace for seven years. Since the Antichrist's father is Satan, why would we expect him to utter the truth? He is incapable of it, so breaking the covenant is a foregone conclusion.

Daniel 9 states that "in the middle of the week" (cf. 9:27) Antichrist breaks his covenant with Israel, turning on them, attempting to completely obliterate them from this planet. Hitler tried it, and numerous others have tried it as well. Antichrist will be the *last* to try it and he will only have some measure of success, but will not prevail.

Regarding 1 Thessalonians, Dr. Olander outlines it in chapters one through three dealing with the rapture (Christ's coming for the Church). In the fourth chapter, we gain more insight into the actual event of Christ's coming to meet His bride in the air. Chapter 5 indicates clearly that Christ delivers the Church from the coming wrath.[54]

One of the key sections is found in 1 Thessalonians 4:17-18 KJV, which states, *"Then we which are alive and remain shall be caught up together with them in the clouds, to meet the Lord in the air: and so shall we ever be with the Lord. Wherefore comfort one another with these words."*

Paul appears to be stating that once this event occurs, it is *then* that the *destruction* of the Day of the Lord begins in earnest. This day can only start, once the Church has been removed. The most interesting thing of all is that Paul points out that people will be saying "peace and safety!" yet it will be at that moment that the Day of the Lord starts, ushering in the most terrible destruction this world has ever known.

Consider something for a moment. IF the Rapture were not to occur until the *end* of the Tribulation, as most Posttribbers believe, then why for goodness sakes, would anyone be saying "peace and safety"? The end of the Tribulation ramps up to a major climax. The Antichrist will have gathered his troops, prepared for battle against the Lord of heaven. How can this be happening (gearing up for war), yet at the same time people are saying "peace and safety"? It cannot be happening.

---

[54] Dr. David Olander ,*The Greatness of the Rapture* (Ft. Worth: Tyndale Press 2009), 102

Peace and Safety? Think Again.

It would appear from the text that just when people start to believe that peace and safety have come to the planet, look out, because far from things becoming peaceful and safe, the Day of the Lord begins, bringing God's judgment and resulting destruction to an unbelieving world. This is the only place that a sense of peace and safety might appear to be happening; at the beginning just after the covenant is signed, sealed, and delivered. Imagine the results of Middle East peace. There will likely be dancing in the streets!

At no other point during the entirety of this seven-year period, will there be any semblance of peace at all. It will certainly not be peaceful just prior to Jesus' return since the Antichrist will be setting himself up to make a stand against the God of heaven.

The Posttribber says that the Rapture occurs at the *end* of the Tribulation period, at the same time Jesus returns to earth in His Second Coming. How is it possible for anyone at that time to say "peace and safety," considering the fact that throughout the preceding seven years, it has been nothing but one plague, pestilence, or war, or something else poured out onto humanity?

Absolutely *nothing* happens *during* the Tribulation, to make people think that peace has finally been achieved. Paul makes this clear. It is *when* people are saying "peace and safety," that the Day of the Lord breaks open onto the earth, like a thief in the night.

The only place this 'peace and safety' could possibly occur is when the Antichrist enters into, or brokers a peace agreement between Israel, other countries in the Middle East and himself. Because this peace has been the most difficult peace to achieve over the centuries, the fact that Antichrist will have achieved it will be reason for celebration. It will be at this point that the Tribulation will officially begin.

Who expects a thief? No one, and in fact, the statement that is heard most frequently after coming home to discover your house has been ransacked is something like, "I never expected this to happen to me." No one expects any type of tragedy. That always happens to the other person!

Think about this though; during a tumultuous time such as now, when everything is looking very bleak for Israel, and any type of peace in the Middle East, it is likely that if someone *can* broker peace in that region of the world, it will be *then* that people will say "peace and safety!" However, the tragedy of course, is that once peace is attained through the signing of the covenant with that Man of Sin, the Day of the Lord will make its debut.

The signing of the covenant with Israel will cause the entire world to dance in the streets! Think of it. Peace will have actually been achieved, so the world thinks. How wonderful it will be, yet this only signals the beginning of the Day of the Lord. The Church will already be gone by that time.

The Reason for the Tribulation
Why does the Tribulation occur at all? Because in signing a covenant with Antichrist, Israel will have effectively entered into a seven-year contract with the devil. God's wrath is then poured out onto an unsuspecting world in retribution for their treatment of Israel and for Israel's continued willful rebellion toward God.

Paul also makes it perfectly clear that true believers will not be overtaken like those who think they are safe from the thief (cf. 1 Thessalonians 5:4). Christians will know that the Day of the Lord is approaching, and folks, it is approaching now.

Everything on the horizon indicates that the Day of the Lord is thundering toward us like a sand storm that obliterates the horizon, engulfing everything in its path. Very few Christians even see it coming though! The ones who do are shouted down, ridiculed and castigated. Authentic Christians will not be caught off guard. Though we are unaware of the exact day and hour that the Tribulation begins, we know by the signs that it is heading our way.

It is clear from 1 and 2 Thessalonians that the Rapture and the Day of the Lord are different events. At the same time, no one knows the day or the hour of His coming for His Church. It will only be after this Rapture has occurred that the Day of the Lord can begin.

Chapter 15

Back to Olivet

AND JESUS ANSWERED AND SAID UNTO THEM, TAKE HEED THAT NO MAN DECEIVE YOU.

©2010 F. DERUVO

O ne of the biggest keys to understanding the time just prior to the beginning of the Tribulation is found in the Olivet Discourse (Matthew 24, Mark 13 and Luke 21). In many ways, this is where all but the PreTrib Rapture position starts to break down. However, like anything else in religion and specifically, Christianity, it honestly depends upon how people interpret various areas of Scripture. Though a number of areas in Scripture cast the light of doubt on the Posttrib Rapture view, Christ's own words in the Olivet Discourse shed a good deal of light on the subject. In order to ascertain the value of His words, it is not even necessary to read between the lines. It *is* necessary however, to understand *fully* what He speaks of when He refers to Noah and Lot, as well as the other areas He broaches. It also needs to be kept in mind that the order of events occurring in the Olivet Discourse is not necessarily chronological. There are a number of things, which are out of order. Interpreting His words, without putting them in the proper order is like trying to do a complex mathematical problem containing a variety of operations, yet doing so without following the Order of Operations.

Noah and Lot

It seems clear from Matthew 24 that Christ describes the time before both Noah and Lot. In many ways, He *seems* to state that life went on "normally" ("eating, drinking, marrying, and being given in marriage"). The trouble though, is that if this were *all* that took place during the lives of these men, would there have been any reason at all for God to send destruction as He did? In Noah's case, the entire world was so bad, that it required God to send a global flood, destroying everything except what was aboard the Ark. In Lot's situation, the two cities – Sodom and Gomorrah – were so obnoxiously sinful that there was nothing left for God to do, except destroy them.

Though in each case, living conditions themselves were good, the people made life exceedingly bad, because they themselves were evil through and through. They could not do anything that was not in some way connected to evil, because evil is what they embraced continually.

In a recent issue of Prophecy in the News, Gary Stearman provides part three of his article, "The Pre-Pre-Tribulation Rapture." In it, he directs his attention to Noah's and Lot's days and the problems of each, with any relationship to the Rapture and Tribulation noted. I realize that many Posttribbers believe that both the deluge that followed God shutting Noah and family up in the Ark, and Lot's escaping to safety, point clearly to a *Posttribulational* point of view, with respect to the

Rapture. I firmly believe they are in error and I will explain why, citing Dr. Stearn's words from his article as well.

Most today, who believe in a PreTrib Rapture (or even disagree with it), know of this entire passage and its use as a proof text for the Second Coming. Most do not see any aspect of any rapture being discussed in the Olivet Discourse. However, people like Dr. Arnold Fruchtenbaum and others, believe that the PreTrib Rapture is clearly in view. Dr. Stearn is in agreement with this position.

Briefly, two reasons are presented, which are said to support the concept that Christ is speaking of the Second Coming, not the Rapture:

"First: contextually, Jesus has been speaking about the Second Coming and since this passage follows that discussion, then, logically, it would mean that He is speaking of the same thing. Second: the 'taking away' of Matthew 24:40-41 is taken to be the same as verse 39, which is a 'taking away' in judgment. Hence, the 'taking away' is in judgment at the Second Coming, and not the blessing of the Rapture."[55]

Again, what has been presented above is the "normal" way of looking at the text in the Matthew 24 passage. However, Stearn notes that Fruchtenbaum points out that Matthew 24:36 *"begins with the word But, which in Greek is* peri de*. The* peri de *construction in Greek is a contrastive introduction of a new subject and, hence, is often translated as:* But concerning (1 Cor. 7:1; 8:1; 12:1; 16:1; 1 Thes. 5:1; etc.)."[56] The point then is simply that while it is agreed that Christ has been discussing His Second Coming *until* this point in the passage, He now moves onto a different subject, which is not at all connected to the Second Coming. The new subject Christ is introducing is the Rapture itself. The problem then involves the chronology of the Olivet Discourse.

---

[55] Gary Stearn *Prophecy in the News* (Oklahoma City: December 2009), 11
[56] Ibid, 11

Because Christ introduces the Rapture *after* His discussion of His Second Coming, this does not, in and of itself mean that the Rapture actually *follows* the Second Coming.

Continuing on, Dr. Stearn points out that in response to the second point (listed above), *"the 'taking away' in verses 40-41 is a different Greek word than the one used in verse 39, and so it need not be interpreted as the same kind of 'taking away.'"*[57] Fruchtenbaum goes into greater detail in his book *Footsteps of the Messiah*.

In commenting then on this, Stearn, in agreeing with Fruchtenbaum, states, *"Verses 40 and 41 (one taken, the other left) translate the word "taken" from the Greek* paralambano. *Unlike the first verb,* airo, *this one means, 'to take to or to take with oneself.' It seems most logical, therefore, to interpret the action o these verses as individuals being 'taken to be with the Lord,' rather than 'taken in judgment.' Interpreted in this way, the ones 'left' are those left behind, to experience judgment."*[58]

Watching, <u>Not</u> Sitting

What must be considered here also is that Jesus Himself tells us that we should be *watching*. Dr. Stearn points out that this word is from the Greek word *"gregoreo, meaning to continually be spiritually alert or awake."*[59] Please note that within the context of the passage, this command is given to the "goodman of the house," not those who do not know Christ at all (the unrepentant sinner), (cf. Matthew 24:43).

We need only take this one step further to prove that Christ cannot be discussing the Second Coming at this point in the passage, and it is something I (and others) have mentioned previously. In Matthew 24:36,

---

[57] Gary Stearn *Prophecy in the News* (Oklahoma City: December 2009), 11
[58] Ibid, 11
[59] Ibid, 11
*see *Between Weeks*, also by Fred DeRuvo for further information on Daniel 9:24-27

Jesus states, *"But of that day and hour knoweth no man, no, not the angels of heaven, but my Father only,"* (KJV). It should be clear where we are going with this. Since Jesus is specifically stating that no one (not even His followers) will know the *day* or the *hour* of His return, it only needs to be asked, how can He be referring to His Second Coming?

Once the Tribulation actually begins, it will be relatively easy for people to determine the *end* of it! Think about it. In Daniel 9:24-27, we read about the time just prior to, between and during the 70th week. Since each week represents a period of *seven years, then we know that the 70th, or final week also extends for a period of seven years. If we know that the Tribulation has a specific start (the signing of the covenant; cf. Daniel 9:24-27), and it will last for exactly seven years, who would not be able to figure out the end?

Those Left Behind

Then someone argues, *"but if the Church is gone, who would be left to actually know about this?"* Good point, and there is an answer. There are multitudes of people who attend churches today who *believe* they are authentic Christians. They may have prayed the "sinner's prayer," or gone forward during an altar call, or did something else to convince themselves that they, in fact, became Christians at one point in time. Unfortunately, many will find out after the Rapture occurs that they were not Christians. Because they are not Christians, they will remain after the Rapture takes place, and they will have the realization that they are not actual Christians. They sat in church, listened to the sermons, maybe even taught Sunday school, but they *never* entered into a living, vital relationship with Jesus Christ. They had the head knowledge, but not the heart knowledge. They knew the truth, but never embraced it.

These individuals will go into the Tribulation with the knowledge that they were only playing church, though they had certainly convinced themselves they were the real deal. All the head knowledge they had stored up over the years will come in very handy during the Tribulation. It will help them become true Christians, and they will lead other people to know Christ as Savior and Lord as well. Beyond this, they will likely begin searching the Scriptures, looking for signs and indications that will provide them with more of an understanding regarding the time they are forced to live through. These folks will be able to calculate seven years from the starting point of the Tribulation. There will be no guessing. It will be seven periods of 360 days each (based on Jewish calculations), and voilá! the Second Coming of Jesus. What could be easier? Even a Neanderthal could do it!

Yet, many insist that this entire section of the Olivet Discourse only references the Second Coming, this in spite of the fact that Jesus states clearly that no one will know the day or hour. If He sincerely means, "no one will know the day or hour," (and there is no reason to believe He is only speaking in general terms), then it follows that *no one will know the day or hour.* Since people will be able to determine the exact day for His Second Coming, then of necessity, He *cannot* be referring to that event when He says no one will know the day or hour, but must be referring to another event altogether. That event is the Rapture.

Another reason why the Rapture cannot occur at the end of the Tribulation is for the same reason we cannot know the day or hour, with reference to the Second Coming. If, as many Posttribbers believe, the Rapture occurs at the same time of Jesus' Second Coming, how can that be if He states we will not know the day or hour? If we can figure out when He will physically return, and the Rapture is said to happen at the same time, then something is wrong somewhere.

All that matters is knowing two things, in order to be able to figure out *when* Jesus will return:

1. The starting point of the Tribulation

2. The exact length of the Tribulation

Once the two items above are understood, a fourth grader could figure out when He will come back. We cannot also look at His words "unless those days were shortened, no flesh would survive" as an indication that He is somehow going to "cheat" the length of the Tribulation, making it shorter than it is stated to be either. This reference of His (cf. Matthew 24:22), simply points out that it will *not* go on indefinitely, but has an actual starting *and ending* point. The ending point of the Tribulation is exactly seven years (by Jewish calculations) after it begins.

Noah Is Removed

Consider Noah and Lot again. Dr. Stearn points out in his article that Noah was not given the command to preach to the people, so that they would repent. This is largely assumed by students of the Bible because of the silence of the Scriptures. It has been assumed that, as Noah built the Ark, he preached to the people to repent because of the coming flood. Part of this assumption is based on Peter's words in his second epistle. There, he states, "*And spared not the old world, but saved Noah the eighth person, a preacher of righteousness, bringing in the flood upon the world of the ungodly...*" (2 Peter 2:5 KJV). We get the idea that if Peter called him a "preacher of righteousness," then he must have actually *told* people what was going to happen. The fact though is that nowhere in God's command did God tell Noah to warn the people. They had to be destroyed because of the corruption of the flesh that existed during that time. God had already decided that He would destroy everything with a global flood and there was no going back. God would start over, using Noah's undefiled human lineage (DNA?), to repopulate the earth.

Since the text of Genesis 6 seems to state that some of the fallen angels made their situation worse after falling by cohabitating with human women (cf. Genesis 6:4), this totally wanton and rebellious act was so

Matthew 24 - Olivet Discourse

"And as were the days of Noah, so shall be the coming of the Son of man,"

Noah	**enters the ark, <u>then</u>**	**God's wrath pours out**

Lot	**heads to the mountains, <u>then</u>**	**God's wrath pours out**

©2010 F. DERUVO

grievous to God that He locked them up, chained in darkness since that time, until future judgment. Peter says, *"For if God spared not the angels that sinned, but cast them down to hell, and delivered them into chains of darkness, to be reserved unto judgment,"* (2 Peter 2:4, KJV).

Getting back to Noah, we know that he built the ark out of obedience. This and this alone may have been why Peter classifies him as "a preacher of righteousness." Noah obeyed God without questioning Him on any point. He heard God, and began doing what God commanded. At the appointed time, after the Ark was finished, and time was up, God told Noah to get into the Ark.

When he, his family, all the animals that God brought to Noah, as well as supplies were safely inside the ark, God closed the door and sealed it from the outside. It was then that the floods occurred, only *after* God's chosen man and his family and all the animals were safely stowed away inside the ark. God's judgment, in the form of His wrath, began once they were all safely inside, and out of harm's way.

Some Posttribbers (and other anti-PreTribbers) come along and say that what the record points to is that God saved Noah and his family *within* the framework of God's judgment. They argue that God did not take them out of His wrath, but merely kept them safe *within it,* as judgment was poured out. However, *what could God have done with them other than this?*

Where Could God Have Put Them?
Aside from completely removing them off the face of the earth, there was no place *on the earth* that Noah could have been placed, which would have enabled him to escape the floodwaters of God's wrath and judgment. God could have had the Ark *hover* above the earth (and in a way He did with the Ark on top of the water that covered the earth), He could have taken them to heaven, or He could have done what He did, kept them safe in the Ark.

Since God made the decision to begin afresh with Noah and his family, it would have been impossible to take them to heaven while His wrath had been spent. To do that would have meant their *death*, since corruption cannot inherit incorruption. Therefore, yes, while God kept them all safe within the ark, as it literally passed through God's judgment on top of the water, the record is clear enough that for all practical purposes, God *removed* them from the situation completely.

It was only after Noah was completely away from the possibility of being touched by God's wrath, did His wrath begin to be poured out onto the earth. This wrath lasted for about a year. Some Posttribbers say that the *very day* that God sealed Noah, his family and the animals into the Ark, His wrath began being poured out. They point to this as a proof for the *Post*trib Rapture because it took place at the same time His wrath occurred. This is doubtful argument. In fact, it is no argument. What it appears that the Posttribber is doing is equating the *beginning* of God's wrath pouring out onto the world as being the same thing as Christ's Second Coming. It is clear though, that Christ does not return until the *end* of the Tribulation, after a period of seven years.

With both Lot and Noah, each was safely removed and *then* God began pouring out His wrath. There was no Second Coming in either of these events, since there had been no First Coming either.

The scenario is more in favor of a PreTrib Rapture position. The reason for this is because once Noah is taken out of the way, it is *then* that God's wrath *begins* to be poured out onto the earth and its inhabitants.

This is exactly what the PreTrib Rapturist says about the Tribulation. The Church is taken out of the way, by being Raptured, or translated up to meet Christ in the clouds, and *then* God's wrath begins to pour out onto the earth and its inhabitants.

Lot is Removed

The same is true of Lot. Genesis 19 includes the narrative of the event that literally shook the heavens and that part of the world. Lot and his wife and daughters were taken out of the way *prior* to God beginning to rain fire and brimstone down on the cities of Sodom and Gomorrah. In this case, it cannot be said that God saved Lot through His judgment, seen in the outpouring of His wrath. Lot and his family were completely removed from the scene.

It seems clear enough that God's wrath occurs *after* He has secured His chosen man in a safe place. For Noah, it was inside the ark. For Lot, it was in the safety of the mountains. For the Church, we will be in the heavens with Christ. Do I hear an "AMEN!"? The only possible argument people can present is by using another definition of God's "wrath" with respect to the Tribulation, and they have tried.

Death is Always Before Us

How many of you can say that you know when you will die? I am not trying to be morbid. I am simply pointing out a fact that we often do not consider. In truth, your death and my death are absolutely and unequivocally imminent. It may happen long before the Rapture ever does. In light of this, how are you living? How am I living my life, every hour of every day? Am I considering each day as if it was my last day on earth? If so, then I should live accordingly, which means living for Christ, not myself. I do not want to stand before him one day only to be exceedingly embarrassed for the way I lived; instead of Christ on the throne, good ol' Fred DeRuvo with his active sin nature had taken over that spot.

Those opposed to the PreTrib Rapture say that this doctrine creates unspiritual, carnal-minded, immature Christians. They say this because they believe the PreTrib Rapture position gives us every reason to stop working, knowing that we will be whisked away in the Rapture before things really get bad. If that is the case, then the very same logic (if you can call it that), applies to the nearness of my death, does it not? I could die today, so it would also be perfectly logical (according to some) to go out and live in the cesspool with the world, enjoying sin for a season. Why not? After all, I will be taking up to heaven at the end of the day in my death, right? For the Christian who lives like that, let it just be said that he needs to take a very serious look at his commitment to Christ. If he is an authentic Christian, then he should want to do the things that glorify the Lord, *all the time*. The idea that because I may die today, I can celebrate by sinning, is ridiculous. By considering the reality of my ever-present death, I take no thought of when I will stand before Christ after death. This makes no sense at all. We have been bought with a price and that price was nothing less than the blood of Christ. He gave His all for us; holding back nothing. How can we do any less?

Becoming a Christian is not how the world views being married. Normally, for the unsaved, worldly individual, one of the "jobs" of the groom's best man is to set up a bachelor party. At times, these parties can become filled with sinful activity. However, it is all in good fun, say many, because this is the groom's last chance to enjoy bachelorhood prior to being married to the "old ball and chain." During that party, a great deal is permissible, by worldly standards. This is essentially the accusation brought against PreTrib Rapturists. Supposedly, because I believe that I will be gone prior to God's wrath being poured out, I can celebrate, enjoy life, and essentially party hearty until I am "called up yonder." How sad and tragic it is that people have gone to this extreme in creating fabricated arguments, which they believe negates the PreTrib Rapture position. It does not do that, except in their minds.

If the thought of being here one moment, and being before Christ the very next moment is not enough to cause people to let go of all earthly things, then something is terribly wrong. For those who have a difficulty believing that the Rapture will occur prior to the Tribulation, then I say fine. They should have no difficulty however, in realizing that death is always one breath away. We need to live like that, because like the Rapture, our death could happen at any moment. Let us endeavor to live for Christ and Him only!

There are only two paths in this life, the wide road that leads to destruction and the narrow road that leads to life eternal. All people are on one of those roads. Which one are you on?

Chapter 16

Out of Patience

©2010 F. DERUVO

Clearly, the world is getting tired of hearing from those of us who believe the Bible to be accurate and literal when it comes to the End Times scenario. Many leaders within the Emergent Church, such as Brian McLaren, Tony Campolo, Rick Warren and others, encourage a disdainful view of Premillennialists in general. They are more interested in placating the world. These individuals have made extremely judgmental and condemnatory statements against those of us who believe the PreTrib Rapture, believing that this type of *negative* viewpoint toward the future simply promulgates more of its kind. Words and phrases like "psychological misfits," "dangerous," "extremely detrimental," and more have been leveled against Premillennialists.

The Opposition

One can only wonder why this proclivity to castigate Premillennialists exists. Upon closer inspection, it becomes clear that the world in general is opposed to believing that one day, the ultimate destruction of this world will take place, executed by God Himself. That is not a pleasant thought. People do not want to consider the reality of hell. It is negative.

We have spent time in this book trying to establish the fact that there are major movements afoot, which have endeavored to eradicate aspects of End Times beliefs that stand in opposition to their ordered goals. The Emergent Church stands opposed to those who believe the literality, veracity, and inspired Word of God.

One particular article states in part, "*The leader of the nation's largest Lutheran has called for a global Christian council to address an 'identity crisis' on how churches interpret and understand the Bible. Presiding Bishop Mark Hanson of the Evangelical Lutheran Church in America ... called for Catholics, Eastern Orthodox, Anglican and Lutheran churches to come together to* **combat** *a fundamentalist-millenialist-apocalypticist reading of Scripture'* [Religious News Service, Aug. 11, 2005; emphasis added].

Prophezine.com, commenting on the article from which the above quote was taken, stated in a recent email update, "*Hanson's request for a group to monitor and expose anti-ecumenists who take the Bible literally carries some weight! His message contains other statements showing his concern about Bible literalists--particularly those who take Bible prophecy seriously and see Israel and the Middle East crisis as an end-times sign post...Bishop Hanson believes that a global ecumenical group made up of Catholics, Eastern Orthodox, Anglicans, and Lutherans is the answer to the crisis he sees."*

We need to consider the dangers inherent within the Emergent Church, Contemplative Prayer, Spiritual Formation and all the rest of the movements and 'isms' alive and well today, it is not difficult to understand that their push is toward ecumenism. The goal is to become "one" with one another. Those who believe that we are heading toward Armageddon are seen, and branded, as fanatics or nut cases.

In fact, in today's pluralistic society, there is less and less room for any individual thought, which does not agree with the unity that ecumenism, seeks to achieve. Opposition cannot be tolerated and for now, though it appears that people who stand opposed to the ecumenical movement, are being labeled these types of things, there will likely come a day (and is now coming), when greater measures will be taken to silence this vocal minority.

Technology Moves It Onward and Upward

It should be understood that this movement toward the full unity of society, has been in place for centuries. However, only in the past century have things really kicked into high gear, and greater technology is one of the things that have put ecumenism into high gear. This technology has in large measure, made this world much smaller. What took days or weeks in the past to get from one side of the world to the other, now takes mere seconds or even milliseconds.

Besides the technology that allows us to send and receive information faster than ever before, an increase in tactical knowledge and defense has also put the world at greater danger of annihilating itself, if not for certain checks that are in place.

However, if the world is literally moving to become united and unified, one must ask what the overall purpose is to achieve that end. If, in fact, the world *can* become one through human effort, what is at the end of that rainbow? What will this one-world look like when we arrive at that point? Moreover, who will be in charge of running it?

Our next chapter will seek to answer these questions, by providing insight from others. Whether you believe it or not is completely up to you. Before rejecting it though, check your emotions at the door.

Chapter 17

Moving Toward The "One"

©2010 F. DERUVO

I t is without doubt clear that the world is moving toward welcoming the last dictator, who, as it happens, will become a global dictator. Fruchtenbaum refers to this kingdom as Absolute Imperialism, led by the Antichrist.[60] How will this happen? It will happen because every major avenue in life – *social*, *religious* and *political* – will come together in the spirit of unity, in order to facilitate a new world order.

Social consciousness, political movements and religious dogma will come together to create the perfect environment for such a leader to

---

[60] See *Footsteps of the Messiah*, by Arnold G. Fruchtenbaum

emerge. Do you think this is far-fetched? Not at all, especially if one considers the fact that within each of these areas, the line of thinking is such that an eagerness for one charismatic leader is at an all time high. All we need to do is look back on the last presidential election. During that time, an almost unrealistic expectation for Barack Obama seemed not only to carry him, but the majority of the nation, like a tidal wave.

A New Messiah?

The news media spoke of him as if he was the Messiah, and voters picked up the chant. Obama became the hope of this nation apparently, so riveted were people to him and his charisma. Of course, there were also those who tried to shout down the others by claiming that there was an excellent chance that President Obama was the Antichrist. The absurdity of this latter accusation became immediately apparent to those who understood Eschatology. Obama is *not* the Antichrist. He simply does not fit the bill.

The most interesting thing remains and that is that President Obama was literally catapulted into the White House because of what many people believed (and still believe), he could accomplish for this nation. There are many reasons why Barack Obama is not the Antichrist; however, the feelings of euphoria that surrounded him, his campaign and his ultimate election to this nation's highest office should be a sign to all of us.

Jan Markell, in one of her emailed ministry updates (dated December 15, 2009, *Understanding the Times*), relates, *"There is much floating over the Internet that Barack Obama is the antichrist. He is not. He simply doesn't qualify. However, in 2009, he fooled the world into believing that he was a world leader. Many Web sites called him "The President of the world," "the messiah," "the world leader," and much more along those lines. He persuaded the masses that he could unite the world, but to do that, America would have to be reduced from a superpower to the same level as Portugal or Brazil.*"[61]

The world watched as the United States elected its first Black president, a man who would not say whether he was a Christian, and while he attempted to sidestep any possible association with Islam he was accused of having, the possible connection dogged his heels. Whether President Obama is a Muslim is debatable, however, he is certainly sympathetic to their cause.

Against Life

Despite the fact that President Obama's voting record on Abortion was atrocious, people seemed very willing to set that aside. This is to be expected from the people who love this world, but the saddest part is that Obama's against-life stance for Abortion seemed not to matter to those who professed Christianity as well.

Many within the secular and "Christian" entertainment world flocked to Obama's side in support of his climb to the top. One cannot help but wonder how professing Christians can support someone who is not only so apparently cavalier and disdainful about life itself, as pertaining to the unborn, but also about his stated penchant to turn the United States into a country espousing Socialism. Yet this is what occurred during the campaign. Well-known singers and musicians within the Christian recording industry offered words of support for Obama, encouraging their fans and audience members to vote for him.

How can this be? How can the world of Christendom become so taken in by someone who is merely *charismatic*, and who delivers a good speech? It happens because those who wind up being swept away in the emotion of the moment end up becoming *deceived* because of it. Their emotion carries them through the decision-making process,

---

[61] Emailed update from Jan Markell's *Understanding the Times*; December 15, 2009

because they lack a solid grounding. They are not in a living relationship with Jesus Christ, though they attend a local church and profess Christianity. They may also lack the maturity that comes from having been a Christian for some time. In these cases then, mature Christians need to be standing alongside these immature Christians, in order to keep them from being carried by emotion, basing their decisions on their emotions, and reaping the consequences of emotions that react the way sand does underneath a house. When the rains come, the house is washed away due to a lack of a strong foundation.

Just Who is Open to Deception?
It is obvious then, that deception can and does take place among those who attend church, professing to be Christians. The Obama election is simply a case in point. What will happen to those professing Christians who are alive when the Antichrist steps onto the world's stage? How will they react then? If the world's reaction to Obama is any indication, they will be taken in by the Antichrist's charm, his charisma, his ability to speak, his seeming sincerity and a whole plethora of other things that will make him stand tall, heads above all other contenders.

With respect to Obama and the coming Antichrist, Jan Markell notes, *"During [Obama's Presidential Election] campaign, he mesmerized the world. Not everyone was fooled, but the world is so longing for a 'man with a plan,' a 'Mr. Fix-it,' that they bought his redistribution of wealth statements and overlooked a dozen dangerous associations and said they just didn't matter because this was the closest the world had come in modern history to this so-called 'President of the world.' Shortly after the 2008 election, Tunisia was just one country of several that headlined the story, 'Today America elects 'the president of the world'."*[62]

For those who still see President Obama as the world's answer to the mess we are in, they are completely missing it. Not only is he not the

---

[62] Emailed update from Jan Markell's *Understanding the Times*; December 15, 2009

world's answer, but neither will the yet-to-be-revealed Antichrist be the world's answer. The world however, will certainly believe that the Antichrist will usher in a new day, a day where problems become outdated with the oft spoken of future Utopia, a thing of the present.

Is Obama Merely a Step Toward?

In truth, we can see in President Obama a dry run for the coming appearance of the last one-world leader, prior to Christ setting up His Kingdom on planet earth, to rule from His "father" David's throne in Jerusalem. Frankly, while I am surprised at the continued support of President Obama, it should *not* surprise me. Long ago, the world rejected God in Jesus Christ. This continued rejection of God forces Him to give people over to themselves.

Markell says it best with her statement, *"There is coming that 'single leader.' Could it be that the world is turning into such a mess so that he -- the antichrist -- will soon come along and say, 'I have the answer to solve all these problems'? Obama's 'messiahship' can't come close to that of the antichrist who will be demonically-appointed to pull a million rabbits out of hats. So what we see now is just a microcosm of what will really happen."*[63]

It only requires Christians to take their blinders off and look around to notice that the world is becoming conditioned to be deceived. However, what is the world being set up to be deceived *about*? It is being set up for deception related to *salvation*. The Antichrist will come along as a charismatic leader, pretending to be filled with altruistic objectives that will usher in true world peace. In essence, he will be filled with objectives that will usher in world *domination*.

After being accepted by the world, through the indoctrination that has occurred long before He came onto the world's stage, the Antichrist will

---

[63] Emailed update from Jan Markell's *Understanding the Times*; December 15, 2009

begin to manipulate the world as a magician manipulates his audience. In essence, a good magician manipulates through deception and misdirection. A good magician has no difficulty in creating for his audience what he wants them to see. His sleight of hand, his misdirection, and even his deception is all for covering his actual purposes.

Antichrist: Master Magician and Snake Charmer

The Antichrist will be a master magician and snake charmer; however, unlike the normal magician who entertains for a few hours, the Antichrist will deceive to *harvest* the souls of men. He will initially appear boasting to have solutions to problems that have never been solved, such as the problem of the continued lack of peace in the Middle East. He will ultimately prove that not only does he *not* care about true peace in the Middle East, but also what he does care about is becoming the one god that this world worships. When he sits down inside the rebuilt Temple, this will not only cause the renewed sacrifices to cease (in fulfillment of Daniel 9), it will make his full intentions known to the world: submit to him, or die. This middle point in the Tribulation is where Antichrist unleashes his supernatural venom on an unsuspecting world.

All of Antichrist's stated goals and objectives will be a smoke screen, designed as subterfuge to lull the world into a peaceful sleep, entrusting all their cares on him. Once he has the world where he wants it, his true malevolence will come to the fore, no longer hidden by the mask of charisma, charm and intellect. He will no longer *need* to hide anything.

However, before the world gets to that point, is there anything in place now that suggests that we *are* actually moving toward this one-world government? I believe there is plenty of evidence, or at least information that appears to be concrete evidence. Let each reader be his or her own judge.

In the book *Behold a Pale Horse*, by the late William Cooper, the litany of items he explains in this one book is astounding. In fact, some areas go beyond the ability to believe because of the claims he makes. Yet, because of the seeming accuracy and inside knowledge that he appears to have possessed (he was killed in 1991, the year after the publication of this book), along with his level intelligence, it is also very difficult to simply set his book aside, believing him to be merely one of those aforementioned nutcases.

Ten Kingdoms Becoming One

The Bible speaks of a worldwide ten-kingdom confederacy that will exist before the final leader of the world steps onto the world's stage. *"As for the ten horns, out of this kingdom **ten kings will arise**; and **another will arise after them**, and he will be different from the previous ones... And he will speak out against the Most High and wear down the saints of the Highest One...and they will be given into his hand for a time, times, and a half a time. But the court will sit for judgment, and his dominion will be taken away, annihilated and destroyed forever. Then the sovereignty, the dominion, and the greatness of all the kingdoms under the whole heaven will be given to the people of the saints of the Highest One; His kingdom will be an everlasting kingdom, and all the dominions will serve and obey Him,"* Daniel 7:24-27 (NASB; emphasis added; cf. also Revelation 13 and 17).

These ten horns, as explained by the angel Gabriel to Daniel, turn out to be the world divided into ten regions or kingdoms. Of course, scholars disagree over exactly which kingdoms are represented here, and whether or not this prophecy has already occurred, or is yet to occur. The truth though seems to point to the yet future, when the entire world will be divided into ten kingdoms. In other words, Gabriel is telling Daniel these kingdoms will be of a global nature, not local.

Out of this global ten-kingdom confederacy, we note that one specific individual arises out of this ten-kingdom confederacy and becomes the *one* ruler over all rulers. Interestingly enough, in Cooper's book, one of the things he discusses is this very subject. In Appendix E labeled "KINGDOMS: CLUB OF ROME'S TEN GLOBAL GROUPS," Cooper highlights what he believes these ten kingdoms will look like, according to the Club of Rome, and these ten groups incorporate all land areas. This report is titled "Regionalized and Adaptive Model of the Global World System," and dated September of 1973.

Of course, Cooper is not the only one who has what he believes to be documented evidence that not only our government, but also all other major governments of the world have been involved in clandestine covert operations, to overthrow the citizenry of the world. Many other authors (some believable, and some not at all believable), have stated as much.

If the push for a one-world government has actually been in the works, continuing to this day from secular sources, then it is understandable why those who believe and espouse Premillennialism are seen more and more as the enemy. We become guilty of stopping, or at least attempting to thwart, the progress that groups like "The Club of Rome" have made and continue to make. If Satan is behind these groups (and there is no reason to believe he is not behind them), then his goal is to bring about a worldwide ten-kingdom confederacy, from which the Antichrist will arise.

The United States Becomes Passé
Also included in Cooper's *Behold a Pale Horse*, is a document titled "A Proposed Constitutional Model for the Newstates of America." This document is just what it sounds like; it is a newly created constitution for the newly created America after Martial Law has been declared. Once Martial Law has been declared, then the current United States

Constitution *will* be set aside. In its place, the United States will become a virtual police state. Your rights, my rights, and all civilian rights will be removed. The U.S. will become totalitarian, as far as the masses are concerned. By the way, it is also interesting to note that this particular document in question was created over a 10-year period at a cost of $25 million taxpayer dollars! One can only wonder when Martial Law is declared in the United States, why our government would choose to go back to *any* form of a constitution. There would be no need and in fact, declaring Martial Law throughout the entirety of the United States merely brings us that much closer to the ultimate ten-kingdom division, and from there, a one-world government.

Moving Toward Socialism

The average individual seems not to notice that more and more of our elected officials are moving this country toward Socialism. President Obama clearly made that statement during his campaign (remember Joe, the plumber?). He actually warned this nation that this is what he planned to do, and yet multitudes voted him into office. He is now making good on those promises.

With most Americans living with their heads in the sand, the massive changes that this country is undergoing, is occurring right in front of them, but no notice is taken (since it is difficult to see anything when your head is buried in sand). Too many people living in this country (and throughout the world), seem to not understand that changes are occurring and will continue to occur until we reach that point, which the Bible speaks of in the book of Daniel as a one-world government. Certainly, it must be of some interest to those who have not studied Eschatology deeply enough, to realize that the plan for this world since the creation of the Illuminati, has been a one-world government.

The problem though is that the authorities have masked this quest in a form that seems not to be so encroaching. They speak of it as a coming time of peace and wonder, a utopia, which will exist once we get our act together. Who does not want this utopia? Too many are willing to give up their rights (and ultimately their lives), in pursuit of this, either by not standing in the way of its approach, or by fighting against it after realizing the true menacing nature of it, as this future utopia continues to arrive.

New Age Monopoly

However, with people who believe that this world is *not* heading toward a fabricated utopia, but a disaster, in which one world leader, having gathered his troops of the earth, will make a last ditch stand against the God of heaven, it only makes sense that these individuals should be silenced.

David Allen Lewis reports in his book *UFO End-Time Delusion* that *"Many in the New Age movement believe that planet Earth is a living being, a goddess named Gaia. They believe that Gaia (Earth) is communicating with 'Ascended Masters of the Hierarchy of the universe.' They believe that soon our 'space brothers' will raise a human leader from our midst whom they will endow with supernormal powers and wisdom. This mean will lead the world to global government and world peace. At some point a world leader will receive power from an alien being known as the 'dragon,' identified in the Book of Revelation as Satan!"*[64]

The New Age does not care about hiding its agenda. It is there for the entire world to see, and the more, the merrier. Go to any number of websites by people like Benjamin Crème, Barbara Marciniak, or others well known within the New Age movement. They have been broad-casting their beliefs that a new world is approaching, which will be led by one individual. Funny how many within Christendom think this to be a fairy tale, yet New Age adherents take it seriously.

---

[64] David Allen Lewis, *UFO End-Time Delusion* (Green Forest: 1997), 16

MODERN DAY BABEL: BUILDING ONE FUTURE

One World
One Religion
One Government

RELIGIOUS	SECULAR	SATANIC
Emergent Church	New Age Movement	Illuminati
Contemplative Prayer	Yoga - T.M.	Masons
Spiritual Formation	Tai Chi	Brotherhoods
Going Green	Meditation	• Skull & Bones
Dominion Theology	UFOology	• Black Nobility
Kingdom Now		Rosicrucianism

All of the above movements and isms share many of the same goals, utilizing similar methods to achieve these goals. The above groups and movements represent only a few of the main ones. There are too many to list.

©2010 F. DERUVO

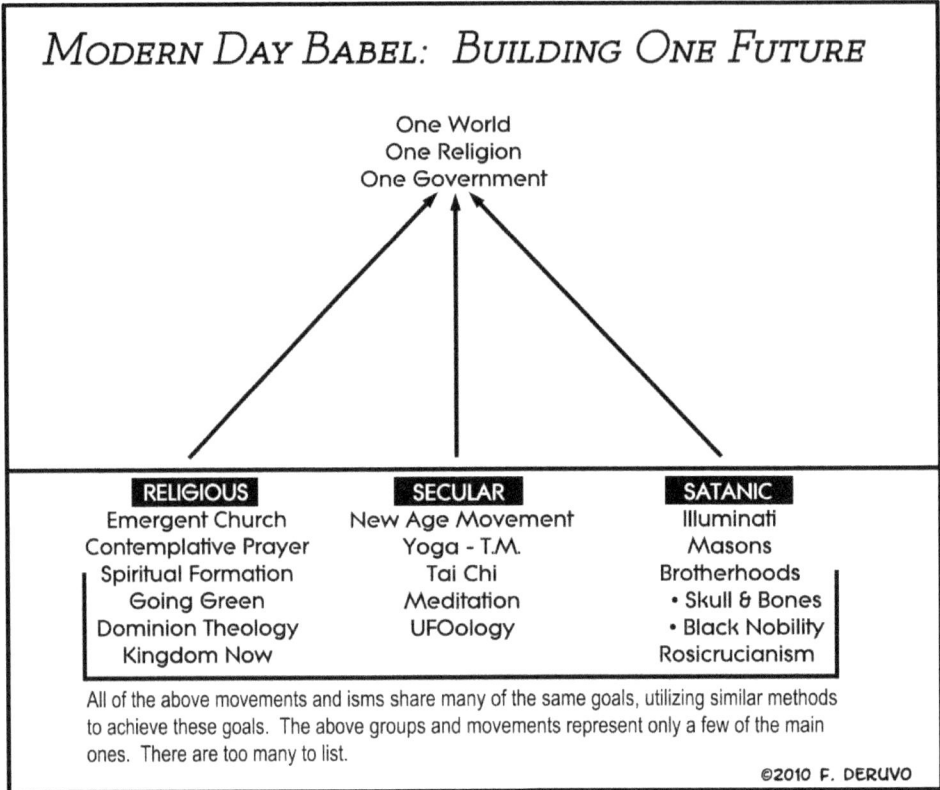

It is interesting how much the beliefs within New Age mirror the Eschatology of conservative Christianity. Yet, we have people like Steve Wohlberg and a multitude of others standing in opposition to the Premillennial, PreTrib Rapture position as being against the Bible.

There are many who pooh-pooh this whole idea of the possibility of a future seven-year Tribulation period. They do not see that right in front of their faces, this idea is coming to fruition. Benjamin Crème has been broadcasting the coming "Maitreya" for the past 20 plus years. This Maitreya (who is apparently already here and wishes only to be known as "Teacher"), will bring the world together in one purpose. He will be able to reveal himself to the world at the right time. Other aspects of the New Age movement indicate the same beliefs in a coming one-world order, which will create for this world, a completely peaceful co-existence for all humankind.

It is not that difficult to see what is happening. Either the devil is wasting a tremendous amount of time trying to get people to believe all these ideas being propagated by the New Age movement (including UFOology, and the like), for something that will not ultimately occur, or he knows it *will* occur, and is merely preparing the people who follow him (knowingly or unknowingly), with a viable explanation. If there is no chance of the world moving toward a ten-kingdom division, which ultimately segues into a one-world government led by one individual, then Satan is expending tremendous energy to accomplish nothing.

Satan Knows More Than We Do

However, it is safe to assume that Satan knows the Bible better than anyone who has lived, is living, or will live (except Jesus). Because he knows and understands it, there is an excellent chance that he is doing all of this behind-the-scenes work, in order to continue to beguile and ultimately deceive those who are his. Certainly, the theologians who firmly believe that the Tribulation occurred long ago wind up playing into his hands and doing some of his work for him, because these individuals come against brothers and sisters in Christ with the name-calling (deceived), arrogant attitudes, and more.

In all seriousness, something is wrong here. Everywhere one looks, it appears as though all avenues are moving toward the same goal and it does not matter which avenue it is, or by what name it is called. It would appear that we have a modern version of Babel being built. However, unlike the one in Genesis 11, which was literally built with physical work and stones, this modern one is being built in the spiritual realm, to be unleashed through the world's systems onto humanity.

There are many who have worked and continue to work against the strategic plans of God, either knowingly or unknowingly. They are deeply involved in overthrowing this nation as their counterparts in other nations work to accomplish the same thing. All of society throughout the globe is working toward a New World Order, ultimately made up of a one-world government. The only question, which remains, is *who* is to be that individual who will control the entire world?

Is it not interesting that what the Bible has taught for thousands of years seems to be coming to fruition by Satan himself, under God's supervision? It is clear that this move toward globalism and ecumenism has been in place for centuries. The Club of Rome's own plan to divide the world up into ten divisions mirrors what Gabriel told Daniel. Yet, some theologians are either unaware of this, or refuse to accept it.

Satan has used his intelligence and deception to replicate what God has decreed will occur, except of course, Satan is trying to do it his way. If the world is moving toward a one-world dictator, then we can assume that other aspects of Daniel 9 are correct, and will come to fruition as well.

It should be easy to see that the plight of the authentic Christian is not left up to chance. Those who actually belong to Christ will be protected by Him. Those who merely profess to know Him, come under no such protection, in spite of what they believe about themselves.

The world is being deceived now, and has been in the throes of deception for some time. The powers of darkness that have created this deception have worked hard and diligently to bring the world to this point. Of course, they work under the supervision of, and within the scope of God's purposes and plan, yet they are on the cusp of foisting their plans onto an unsuspecting world.

It is Another "Gospel"
The deception that is overtaking the world and even swallowing up the theology of many churches has absolutely nothing to do with a wrong

view of Eschatology. It has *everything* to do with a wrong view of salvation.

While there are many like Steve Wohlberg who seem unable to hold themselves in check before calling the PreTrib Rapture position *deception*, in truth, this coming one-world order includes a new religion. This new religion is nothing more than another "gospel." It is another gospel because the authentic Gospel of Jesus Christ is not included. What *is* included is the concept that all people are part of the divine order. Humanity merely needs to unlock its collective divinity and we are well on our way to bringing about our own utopia. This is why the world needs one world leader, someone who can lead the entirety of humankind toward realizing its own divine nature.

This coming world leader will dominate the world not with military might (at first), but with charm, charisma, intellect and a sense of the divine. The entire world will clamor after this individual. Go to any New Age meeting, or read any of their books and they all state the same thing.

Read just about any book by some of the more well known leaders within the Emergent Church. Where is the Gospel of Jesus Christ? It is absent. Platitudes, positive thinking, good wishes with a few Scripture verses tossed in for good measure are substituted for the real Gospel. The gospel that is being pushed through Emergent Church venues is no gospel at all. However, what is being taught, because it is being taught in churches, or during worship services, or written about by so-called Christian authors, is accepted without so much as a question.

Both Christians and Christian posers are being inundated with New Age philosophies and mysticism, under the guise of Christianity. It is becoming the norm and those who are not part of this norm are increasingly being seen as the enemy.

Those who do not understand that salvation is found in Jesus Christ and in no other Person, and that salvation is sure and eternal, are at serious risk. They are at risk of being eternally deceived, because these individuals are tossed to and fro by every wind of doctrine, with no sure footing at all (cf. Ephesians 4:14). While believing that they are authentic Christians, they may wake to find themselves deceived beyond help and hope, unaware that the salvation they believe they have, is nothing more than feelings of hope in someone who offers the exact opposite.

I think it is interesting that many within the Church stand on the sidelines, condemning the PreTrib Rapture position, and castigating those who believe and espouse it. At the same time, Satan seems to be hard at work bringing about the very thing that the PreTrib Rapturist speaks of, based on Daniel 9. Are these naysayers doing the enemy's work for him? It certainly seems possible.

Arguing About the PreTrib Rapture is Only a Smoke Screen
Does anyone else see how all the chatter and discussion (or even arguing about) the PreTrib Rapture *sidesteps* the real issue? If I believe that the Lord is going to Rapture His Church prior to the beginning of the Tribulation, this does not, create a sense of "*Whew! I do not have to worry about how I live, nor do I have to take my relationship with Jesus seriously because He is going to save me from the wrath to come!*" How ridiculous is that?

For those professing Christians who actually believe as just stated there is a serious question as to the validity of their Christianity. An authentic Christian is not concerned about what may occur in our lives, sent at God's discretion. The authentic Christian is concerned with living *for* God and His glory. The authentic Christian is prepared to live through persecution if this is what the Lord decrees. The authentic Christian is fully willing to submit himself to whatever God's plan calls for in this life, because he knows that God sends everything for only two reasons, 1) His glory, and 2) the Christian's growth and maturity.

It is to this end that each true Christian endeavors to die to self, submitting himself to all aspects of God's chosen will for him. To do any less is to keep Self on the throne, denying God full access. This cannot be and this is what must be guarded against.

We must say with Paul, for me to live is Christ and to die is gain. That should be our battle cry for daily living. It is for this end that we are Christians, and it is for this reason that He called us to become part of His family.

War Goes Nuclear?

Just today, I read in an email bulletin from Aaron Klein that Israel and Arab countries are in the midst of planning war with Iran. Why? Because of the threat posed by Iran's nuclear program. There are wars and rumors of wars to be sure. Beyond this, are we closing in on a Northern Invasion spoken about in Ezekiel 39?

I sometimes wonder what it will take (besides the Rapture itself), to convince some of these theologians who are totally at odds with the Premillennial perspective, that their position may not be as meritorious as they believe it to be.

For those whose efforts seem to be motivated by a sense of urgency regarding what they consider the errant view of PreTrib Rapturism, I would humbly ask that they reconsider their opinions.

Chapter 18

Enough!

Not long ago, I read the following comment on an Internet forum dedicated to the Posttribulation argument and to proving that the PreTrib Rapture position is absolutely and unequivocally wrong:

"Should the pre-trib view be a deal breaker, as far as joining a church, for those of us who believe in a post trib gathering of Christians?"

My Rant – Take it or Leave it

Brilliant! What verve! What inspiration! Of *course,* everyone should steer well clear of ANY church, which professes a PreTrib view of the

Rapture! I mean, come on, let's think about this rationally. Since most anti-PreTrib Rapturists firmly believe that those who believe and espouse the PreTrib Rapture are deceived, the answer to the above question is a no-brainer. If the PreTrib Rapture position is one that is born of deceit, from the "pit of hell" itself, then how many other doctrines within that particular local body are also contaminated with deceit?

In fact, if one seriously considers the situation, then how can a person who is so deceived by something "man-made" like the PreTrib Rapture, not be affected in all other areas, no? It is said, that the PreTrib Rapturist is doomed to hell, because the PreTrib Rapturist who is alive when the Tribulation begins, will likely be duped into accepting the mark of the beast. We all know that those who receive this particular mark have essentially given their souls over to the devil, to receive the same punishment he will receive.

Based on this then, how would it be possible for a PreTrib Rapturist to see his way clear to the truth in any doctrinal area? If he does find the truth, it must surely be accidental, because the deception that clouds his thinking regarding the Rapture obviously influences every area of his life, theologically. The fact that the PreTrib Rapturist believes that Jesus is very God, in full humanity, and that Jesus shares two complete natures, is an accident in his thinking. The fact that this same PreTrib Rapturist believes that Christ was born of his mother, Mary, a virgin at the time of conception is predicated upon nothing more than happenstance.

The PreTrib Rapturist who believes that Jesus always was and always will be God, the Son (the second Person of the Trinity, made up of three individual Personalities, all equal, with different roles), has only arrived at this conclusion because of the fact that the stars and constellations came together one day and this bit of light shined into the darkness of his soul.

It is clear – if one listens to all the continuing rants by anti-PreTrib Rapturists – which I, as a PreTrib Rapturist, do not come by my understanding of Scripture honestly. In fact, because I am deluded by the deceptive nature of the PreTrib Rapture, it is a wonder that I can speak any truth at all regarding Scripture. The fact that I do not simply melt into some form of false puddle of humanity when I begin to open my mouth, is testament only to the fact that God, who has tremendous pity on me, allows me speak, and every once in a while, I manage to say something that contains some semblance of truth in it.

It Has Gone Far Enough!

Look folks, the absurdity of this situation has gone way too far, and I would personally like to extend my thanks and gratitude to Dave MacPherson and his followers, for providing new meaning to the words "gracious," "loving," "charitable," and "considerate." Without Mac, where would we be? Instead of dealing with important issues like evangelization, equipping the saints, growing in Christ and more, Christians (professing and authentic), across the globe have become divided over one issue and one issue only, which is *the timing of the Rapture*. How absurd is that? Thank you, Dave, for not following your own father's advice, with respect to entering into dialogue and debate with those with whom you are opposed.

MacPherson has in fact, actually helped to change the meaning of two words: *apostasy* and *heresy*. In the past, these words were almost exclusively used with reference to teaching that attempted to *mitigate* or *add to*, the *doctrine of salvation*. Since Dave's eight insightfully useless books on the "secret" (shhh!), origins of the Rapture, it has become common to toss either or both of these words at unsuspecting PreTrib Rapturists. Why? Because far too many people believe that Dave MacPherson, without equivocation, has proven his point, you know that the PreTrib Rapture was created by men. Two men in fact, are credited with this humungous and heinous deception – J. N. Darby, and C. I. Scofield. Now because all who believe Dave's "findings," conclusively believe the implications of these findings – that the PreTrib Rapture originated deceptively, those who believe the aforementioned proven-to-be-false-through-deception PreTrib Rapture are also deceived. Yea and verily, I say unto thee, be gone thou person of deceptive nature!

Since the deceptive nature of the PreTrib Rapture is a foregone conclusion to many, resulting in the belief that those who believe it and espouse it are also deceived, then the demeanor of these same individuals toward PreTrib Rapturists is one of arrogance. I am sorry to say that, but it is true, and I have even had a few Posttribbers admit it to me.

The question at the beginning of this chapter posed by a Posttribber (who shall remain nameless), proves the point. So concerned is he of the evil and sordid nature of the PreTrib Rapture, that one of the most pressing questions for him is whether he should attend a church in which every other doctrinal position might be right, yet these folks believe in the PreTrib Rapture. At this moment, I understand he is looking for dust to walk through, in order to be able to shake it from the soles of his work boots.

Frankly, this whole situation has become ridiculous, and it does not seem to be winding down any time soon. It is a case of someone who proved *nothing*, being believed by tons of folks, because either,

1. *They already believed the PreTrib Rapture was incorrect, or*
2. *They might have called themselves PreTrib Rapturists, but did not know enough about it to be able to prove it from Scripture*

Mac's books have stretched truth, revised history, ignored pertinent facts and downplayed anything found within Scripture that intimates a PreTrib Rapture perspective. Yet this perspective, so eagerly embraced by those opposed to the PreTrib Rapture, has merely put the PreTrib Rapturist on the defensive and at the same time, made the Posttribber appear to be the real victim. After all, talk to nearly any Posttribber and they will tell you the following:

- *The PreTrib Rapture position was completely unheard of in the early church*
- *Those who believe and espouse the PreTrib Rapture will be completely unprepared for the coming Tribulation*
- *The PreTrib Rapturist is deceived and deluded, therefore is a spiritual infant, if saved at all*
- *There is a good likelihood that PreTribbers alive when the Tribulation begins, will completely lose sight of any truth they now possess, and be overtaken by the deceptive nature of the Antichrist, which will lead to their receiving the mark of the beast, sealing their eternal destination*

It goes on and on and on and on, and yet it reminds me of a situation, which happened to me when I was in the 7th grade. Though I was the victim, the truth was changed to a lie and I became the perpetrator.

The Victim Becomes the Victimizer

In between classes, I sometimes purchased a small bag of popcorn. Money was tight, so I could not do this daily of course, but when I could, it was a nice treat. One day, a classmate of mine that I hardly knew decided it was fine for him to simply help himself to a handful of my popcorn; the popcorn that I paid for and had the sole right to eat or share, at my discretion. He came up to me, helped himself and was gone before I realized what had just occurred. This happened again a few days later, which really annoyed me, but again, I was too shocked to say anything. Finally, the third time I was ready. He came up, reached out his hand, and before he could help himself to one, golden-popped kernel, I said, *"Hey! Knock it off! Stop stealing my popcorn!"*

He immediately giggled a bit in embarrassment, then without taking any popcorn, simply moved off.

Paying the Piper

I felt good. I had stood up for myself and won, without a fight, and things did not get ugly. As it turns out, the very next class is where this particular classmate joined me. As we were preparing for class, this young man said, "DeRuvo wouldn't let me have any of his popcorn!" I was dumbfounded and didn't say anything, because I was incredulous at the accusation. Then I started hearing this phrase, "Fred's a racist." Why? Because this particular young man was Black (which is how you respectfully referred to an individual of that ethnicity during that era), and who it was easy enough to accuse me of being racist, even though I had simply tried to protect what was mine. Then a few other classmates picked up the chant. I glanced at the teacher, who did nothing. One individual, whom I thought had been an actual friend turned around and gave me an ugly look as I tried to explain. I was interrupted by this "friend" who told me in no uncertain terms to "shut up!" Again, the teacher did absolutely nothing and as I glanced over at the student who had started it all, he simply sat there with a smug look on his face. While I had originally been the *victim*, he had managed to turn it around so that it actually looked as if he was the victim! I simply sat there wondering how that happened.

To me, this is exactly what Dave MacPherson has done. Though many extremely qualified individuals have taken the time to respond to his unqualified and bogus charges, it has done little good. The story of how poor little Margaret MacDonald created the PreTrib Rapture (never mind that a careful reading of her "vision" indicates it to be actually a Posttrib Rapture), and then two grown men got together and managed to bamboozle the entirety of the evangelical church at the time, is repeated by many throughout the world.

Because Dave MacPherson said it, and gave reason to believe what people have always wanted to believe about the PreTrib Rapture, people swallowed it, completely. It is now permanently embedded in the landscape of church history and the fact that it is so full of holes, it makes Swiss Cheese look like a solid brick of cheddar, has no affect on those who put stock in the story. These folks are not interested in anything, but continually pointing out the deceptive nature of the PreTrib Rapture. Yes, I am annoyed, solely because they are doing the very thing they charge the PreTrib Rapturist with having done: taking someone's word for it.

Think about something for a moment. As a PreTribber, I could be right-on about all other biblical doctrines and theology, but the fact that I believe and espouse the PreTrib Rapture, that and that alone could mean the difference between salvation or not. Don't think so? If not, then why did this person even ask the question to begin with? If I am right across the board about all other important doctrines, why does the timing of the Rapture even come into play?

A Bit of Tongue in Cheek
You see, this individual is under the delusion that a correct (or not) belief, regarding the timing of the Rapture has something to do with a person's salvation. What could be more ridiculous? Did you not notice in the synoptic gospels that Jesus spent 13 chapters in each book, reminding His disciples, and reminding them again, that in the Last Days, wolves would come, attempting to enter the Church. He warned His followers that these people would be right about everything, except the timing of the Rapture. Because of that, other Christians should be wary, to say the least. PreTrib Rapturists should be kept at arm's length, because the very delusion and deception they live under could easily affect the entire body of that particular local church, in spite of the fact that they are correct about everything else!

In fact, please recall with me the hours that Jesus hung on the cross. Here the two malefactors – one on each side – ridiculed and reviled Him. Then, unexpectedly, one of the two men changed his mind about just who this Jesus really was (this is called repentance), and actually wound up humbling Himself before the Lord of Life. Because of this newfound humility, he made only one tiny request of Jesus, which was that He remember him (the thief), when He came into His kingdom.

We know the story, don't we? Jesus painfully turned to him and said, *"Verily, verily, unless you disavow the PreTrib Rapture position that will come to the fore in the 1800s, you cannot inherit the kingdom of God!"* We know the rest of this tragic story. That man, who had placed all of his unfulfilled hopes in Jesus, now turned his head in away in abject sorrow. For alas, he was, a PreTribber.

The utter stupidity of the question at the beginning of this article is one, which reminds me of how the media deals with Conservatives. If a Liberal is caught in some scandal, they charge Conservatives with dirty politics, and the media have a field day, rushing to the side of their wounded Liberal (Socialist) benefactor and friend. How DARE anyone accuse Ted Kennedy of covering over the death of Mary Jo Kopechne! How DARE a conservative come out in favor of Sarah Palin, charging that President Obama, as he ran for office, surreptitiously referred to her as a "pig," and refused to apologize for his offhand remark. The mistake was the conservative's interpretation, not President Obama's actual verbiage!

The PreTribber is Wrong and Deluded, Right?
This is how the PreTribber is treated by Posttribbers. We are wrong, we are deceived, we are deluded, and we are even in danger of losing our salvation. Should a Posttribber even deign to worship alongside someone who is obviously so misguided, their salvation could very well become jeopardized.

So here was Joe Posttribber asking whether it was SAFE to attend a church, which according to the way he thinks, was right about all major doctrines, but whose attendees clung deplorably onto a "theory" that was fully man-made, proved to not be in the Bible, and, was obviously a matter of deceptive origin in the first place! This kind of thing could result in the disruption of the space-time continuum. About now, we can expect Paul to chime in with, "Brothers, this ought not to be!"

I cannot help but find it fascinating that alleged Christians have sunk so low, as to refer to other brothers and sisters in the Lord, as *deceived* and *deluded*, possibly in danger of falling completely off the narrow path of salvation, because of their belief that the Lord will return to Rapture His Bride BEFORE the beginning of the Tribulation. Can anything be more asinine than this? Does this not reek of the powers of darkness and their involvement?

Eight and Counting?

One manufactured argument after another has been foisted upon unsuspecting Christians, in attempts to challenge and disprove the PreTrib Rapture. In the beginning, it was thought that one or two rebuttals to Dave MacPherson would have done the trick, but who would have thought he would have eight books' worth of un-insightful garbage to write about? Many Posttribbers were completely sold on Mac's ideas the moment his first book hit the shelf, in the early 70s. Why? Because they already believed the PreTrib Rapture was wrong and Mac simply gave them more ammunition. Never mind that he proved nothing. That did not matter.

Since then, the very mention of the PreTrib Rapture recalls the fiery one-word retort of Posttribbers (and others) everywhere: APOSTASY! This is stated much the way liberals denounce anyone who would deign to protest abortions on demand, while at the same time, announcing their pity for the poor, unwed mother, of whom the government should care for, or in our case, the PreTrib Rapturist.

If truth were told, with everything that is happening in this world right now, and its unchangeable direction toward a one-world, Absolute Imperialism, how could the PreTrib Rapture position even *remotely* be part of this deception? It is absurd to consider it because of all that is being accomplished by the enemy of our souls to establish himself as god. He is even now, bringing things to the point of being able to reveal the Man of Sin, the Antichrist, who will reign supreme on this planet for a period of seven years.

Many satanically inspired groups throughout the world believe firmly that their actions of satanic worship are bringing the Antichrist that much closer to appearing on the world's stage. They long for it and endeavor to bring it about. New Agers also believe that their "harmonic convergence" will usher in the Maitreya for the same purpose. At least the Satanists are more honest about whom it is that will be appearing. Unfortunately, the Satanist wrongly believes that the god they worship – Satan – is much more powerful than the only wise God, who happens to be Savior in offering salvation to humanity. They need Jesus.

Please take the time to consider all that is going on behind the scenes and in spiritually dark places. Certainly, all of it is at God's discretion, but the truth remains that all malevolent beings work to bring a time of unprecedented evil upon this world. God will use it for His wrath, seal after seal, bowl after bowl, trumpet after trumpet, as He pours out His divine wrath on a planet that has resolutely refused to bow the knee to Him.

God has been more than patient, more than compassionate, and more than loving, as His message of salvation has been extended to the individuals on the earth for generations. The deception that is engulfing this planet and the people living on it will continue to be believed and embraced by multitudes due to the strong delusion that God Himself sends. These people are and will continue to believe THE lie; the lie that states salvation is found in another, and not in Jesus Christ. That is *the lie*. That is *the deception*. That is what every fiber within the satanic community has been working toward, and it would appear that the climax is soon to occur. None of this deception is predicated upon anything to do with the Rapture, much less the PreTrib Rapture position.

It is the Appearance

All groups, movements and isms that are outside of authentic Christianity (especially those masquerading as Christianity), are part of the deception. Satan has mastered the art of creating what many different groups and individuals need. To the Satanist, he appears as someone to be directly worshipped. To the mystic, he poses as someone who yearns for world peace. To the religious mystic, he pretends that all roads lead to God.

Satan has not been sitting on his rear end, doing nothing for the past 2,000 years. He has been busy doing whatever he can to bring his one message of false salvation to the masses, and he has changed the way it looks according to those he is dealing with at the time. Because of that, there is virtually something for everyone, but the underlying message is always the same. The packaging looks different from one method to the other, but the message that Satan is communicating *never* changes. The basic ingredients do not change, just the wrapping.

The wrapping draws people into the mix and can change to suit the need. It can look like Benjamin Crème, Barbara Marciniak, or an alien from outer space, or a leader in the Emergent Church like Brian McLaren, or Tony Campolo. Satan has no qualms about using a variety of different people from all walks of life to achieve his goals. He has had thousands of years of practice, so he knows what works and what does not work. Practice makes perfect, however, in his case, we know he will ultimately fail.

When someone is accused of being heretical, that person becomes a leper of immense proportions. For many people, it does not matter whether the PreTrib Rapture position has been proven heretical. *"Dave MacPherson said it. I believe it. That settles it!"* is the mantra. Yet, these very same people decry the PreTrib Rapturist's tendency to listen to "man," as if going to Young's Literal Translation, or Wuest's Word Studies puts them on the lowest rung of the religious totem pole. Like wealthy Liberals, who drive their Cadillac SUVs, and live on multi-acred estates in the wealthiest areas of the United States, they decry all the "victims" in society. Never mind that their victims are usually self-made.

Single mothers, and others who make selfish choices (they need someone who will love them unconditionally…until they get tired of raising them, or the government check stops coming), apparently deserve to receive from the government (taxpayer) all the benefits of a corporate CEO. They should not go without, because they were apparently powerless to do anything for themselves other than hop in bed with someone they may have hardly known, without any type of protection whatsoever. We must help them because of the selfishness and stupidity that led them to the point of having children out of wedlock. It is not for us to judge, but to help!

Victims in Name Only
The problem is that the people who believe they are actual victims are victims in *name* only. In that sense, the Posttribbers (and other anti-PreTrib Rapture people), have made *themselves* victims by proclaiming on one hand that their job is to *free* the PreTribber from his delusion, and on the other hand, protect the Church from apostasy the PreTribber allegedly espouses!

Because of the way our friend at the beginning of this chapter thinks (with multitudes who would agree with him), it is becoming - sadly enough - dangerous to be a PreTrib Rapturist. The saddest part is that these same Posttribbers and other anti-PreTrib Rapture people apparently do not see the real problem in the church today.

Christians need to realize exactly *who* the enemy is and then we need to decide *what* to do about it. I can tell you that the enemy is *not* the person who believes the PreTrib Rapture. The enemy is the same enemy that the Church has always had – Satan himself and his goal, in case we have forgotten, is to *keep* people *from* true salvation, and to overthrow God's rule.

The Deception of the End Times

Whether or not people believe in a PreTrib, Posttrib, No-Trib Rapture or something else entirely, has no impact on the truth of *salvation*. The deception of the End Times is concerned with replacing the true Gospel of Jesus Christ with *another* gospel, which is not another gospel at all.

While people seem to enjoy making the statement that the PreTrib Rapture is born of deception, the actual truth is that it is not. While some make a connection between the PreTrib Rapture and salvation, no real connection exists. Yet, people continue to claim that the PreTrib Rapture is deceptive in nature, in spite of the fact that Dave MacPherson proved nothing, yet people act as if he did.

Since these same individuals who believe the PreTrib Rapture to be deceptive in nature, defer to MacPherson and his unproven theories, they believe the oneness is on him, not them. After all, they are merely deferring to his "research," which to them, indicate a clear-cut questionable origin and cover up, related to the PreTrib Rapture position.

If people will take the time to stop and think about what actually constitutes deception in Scripture, they will find that it does not refer to areas of Eschatology. Paul fought against a number of deceptions – heresies – that existed in the early church. He fought against people who claimed that Jesus did not come in the flesh. He argued in favor of keeping salvation pure and undefiled against those who wanted to add requirements like circumcision to it.

Paul took people to task over their inability to take their commitment to Christ seriously. The types of heresies that existed within the early church continue to exist today. These deceptions are related directly to either the Person of Jesus Christ, or the salvation that He purchased on our behalf.

When Paul speaks about a coming "great falling away," that he said would occur in the End Times, just prior to the revealing of the man of sin, some people automatically assume that he is referring to something other than those heresies, which are directly related to salvation. This is a false assumption though, because Paul is specifically referring to that which pulls people *away from Jesus Christ*.

Paul speaks of a falling away from the faith. The *only* thing that pulls people away from the *true Gospel* is *another gospel*. Satan has been involved in creating this charade since the beginning of time. He has worked through individuals to create false salvation theories and these false theories normally *change* the method of salvation that has been established by Jesus Himself. These false theories of salvation always wind up *adding* requirements to salvation, or changing it completely by redirecting the focus to something or someone else.

Our (Alleged) Intrinsic Divinity
Within the New Age movement for instance, the "theology" is such that people are taught that the divine exists within them. What is needed is for people to unlock the hidden and intrinsic divinity that already exists.

Once this is done, then New Age adherents are on their way to creating their own reality, very much like the underlying teaching throughout the Matrix movie trilogy. This is no different from what the Tempter told Adam and Eve – that they would be like God, once their eyes were opened, able to create their own reality. The New Age movement offers the same promise, using different verbiage.

Various movements within Christendom promise a variety of things, and de-emphasize the reality of salvation that is only found within Jesus Christ. The Emergent Church is one such movement that seeks to establish an atmosphere where questions are encouraged, but solid (dogmatic), answers are not. Dogmatism about certain beliefs long held within Orthodox Christianity – the deity of Christ, salvation through Him and Him alone, the Triune Godhead, the virgin birth, Christ's death *and* resurrection – are discouraged, replaced with an opportunity to ask questions and allow people room to interpret God and Scripture the way they believe it should be interpreted...*for them*.

In an environment like the one described above, it should be readily obvious to see how it would be relatively easy to move away from Christ, because of the de-emphasis on authentic salvation. Whether it is within the New Age movement itself, or the New Age movement that has firmly established itself within the visible Church, the salvation preached is completely different from that preached within the authentic Church.

Why do these things work at all? Why did Adam and Eve give into the temptation in the first place? It comes back to emotions. Satan made Eve *feel* as though she and Adam were missing something. She decided that they were in fact, missing something, and following Satan's advice would provide it.

It Has Everything to do with Feeling
Why do people give into all types of sin? It normally has to do with the

way a temptation makes someone *feel*. Lust is difficult to ignore, because of the feelings it stirs up. Many other types of temptations, including a desire for riches, fame or something similar, all stem from how fulfilling those temptations will make us feel. Why do people become actors? For the most part, it has to do with ego. While many individuals are talented – often extremely so – the need for recognition and applause is often what drives them. Take away the audience and no actor is inclined to act.

Why do people go into politics? While at first, it may appear to them that their reasons are altruistic, it is not too long before the corruption of politics grabs hold and they quickly realize that getting a bill passed has more to do with whose back should be scratched.

The truth of the matter is that most temptation hits us in our emotions. We *want* to feel good. We need to feel fulfilled. Instead of applying ourselves to studying God's Word and praying, we prefer to go to a meeting where miracles are allegedly being doled out.

Instead of taking our commitment to the Lord seriously, we would rather attend a church that uses loud rock music as part of their worship service. That makes us feel good. We enjoy it. Never mind that God might be finding no pleasure in it at all. What counts is how we feel about it.

The absolute truth of the matter is that most of the time, people become hooked by emotions, not knowledge, or a deepening understanding of our relationship with Christ. We want to feel it, to see it, to experience it. This drives us to fulfill this desire in many places, like the Charismatic movement, or this faith healer or that one. We go to another worship service because we heard some person calling himself God's Bartender is there.

Satan takes advantage of our weaknesses when it comes to our emotions. Satan does what he can to capitalize on the fact that we too often give in to our emotions. What other reason is there for why people find themselves attending an Emergent Church, or finding great solace in a book like *The Shack*? Because we know God is supernatural, we believe that our experience with God needs to be experienced in a supernatural way. If not, we are convinced (either by the devil or ourselves), that we have not truly "found it." We will continue looking, by migrating from one group to another. Eventually, we will find something that we connect with, and at that point, all the doctrine we have learned, understood and believed flies out the door, in favor of what we feel.

What I believe about the Rapture has *nothing* to do with my salvation. The synthetic argument that because I believe the Rapture will occur, transferring me instantly to heaven prior to the wrath of the Tribulation, I will be left completely unprepared for that Tribulation period (when the Rapture does not occur before the Tribulation), is nonsense. While it sounds spiritual, and while it appears at first glance to be meritorious, it is not.

Death or Rapture – It's All the Same
My belief that Jesus will Rapture me to heaven before the Tribulation begins, is on the same level as my belief that my physical death could occur at any moment. The essence of both of these beliefs is that I am always one heartbeat away from being ushered into His presence.

While I may live to be 100, I may also die before I finish writing this book. If you are reading this, neither my death nor the Rapture has occurred and, coincidentally, neither has your death. I am fine with that either way, because ultimately, I know that I *will* be with Christ and He will bring me home to Him at the exact moment I am scheduled to go there; whether by death or through the Rapture.

Authentic Christians need to stop calling each other "deluded," "deceived," "heretical," and the like, unless it has to do with the preaching of another gospel. It serves no purpose at all; no *good* purpose at any rate. Besides making Satan laugh with glee, it only saddens and grieves the Lord. Maybe that is the problem though. Maybe authentic Christians are not the ones calling others deluded and deceived. Maybe *professing* Christians are creating the problem.

There are people who need to hear the Gospel of Jesus Christ. They are lost and they are on the highway to hell. We need to introduce them to the *only* One who can do something about their lost condition, and that is the Person of Jesus Christ.

Being a Christian is not easy-believism. It is *entering* into a relationship with God Most High! Wow, think about that. A relationship is not static. It is a living, growing entity, which causes us to change and grow over time. People need to know about salvation, that it is not saying a few "magic" words and then, voila! Being an authentic Christian means to understand that if we are going to receive salvation, we then enter into a relationship with Jesus that continues into eternity. It means agreeing to give up our wants, replacing them with His wants.

Nowhere that I am aware of, does the Bible teach that believing in a PreTrib Rapture adds or takes away from salvation. It is not heresy. While it might ultimately prove to be the incorrect view, it will still not be heresy.

So, let's stop destroying one another with words, drop the accusatory language, and get out and witness to the lost. In case there is a question, the lost is the person who does not KNOW Jesus Christ because they have never entered into that vital, soul-saving relationship with Him. That needs to change and only Christians can provide the truth that will allow that situation to change. Whether they listen or not, they *must* hear the Gospel. The rest is up to God Himself.

NOTES

Resources for Your Library:

BOOKS & DVDs:

- The Antichrist and His Kingdom, by Thomas Ice
- Basis of the Premillennial Faith, The, by Charles C. Ryrie
- Biblical Hermeneutics, by Milton S. Terry
- The Case for Zionism, by Thomas Ice
- Charting the End Times, by LaHaye and Ice
- Christian and Social Responsibility, The, by Charles C. Ryrie
- Church in Prophecy, The by John F. Walvoord
- The Coming Cashless Society, by Thomas Ice and Timothy J Demy
- Dictionary of Premillennial Theology, Mal Couch, Editor
- Dispensationalism Tomorrow & Beyond, by Christopher Cone, Ed
- Exploring the Future, by John Phillips
- Footsteps of the Messiah, by Arnold G. Fruchtenbaum
- Future Israel (Why Christian Anti-Judaism Must Be Challenged), by E. Ray Clendenen, Ed.
- The Great Tribulation, Debate with DeMar and Ice (DVD)
- Interpreting the Bible, by A. Berkeley Mickelsen
- Israelology, by Arnold G. Fruchtenbaum
- Moody Handbook of Theology, The by Paul Enns
- Mountains of Israel, The, by Norma Archbold
- Pre-Wrath Rapture Answered, The, by Lee W. Brainard
- Prolegomena, by Christopher Cone
- Promises of God,The, a Bible Survey, by Christopher Cone
- So Great Salvation, by Charles Ryrie
- There Really Is a Difference! by Renald Showers
- Things to Come, by J. Dwight Pentecost
- The Truth Behind Left Behind, by Thomas Ice and Mark Hitchcock
- Truth War, The, by John MacArthur
- What on Earth is God Doing? By Renald Showers

Resources for Your Library (cont'd)

INTERNET:

- Ariel Ministries   www.ariel.org
- Berean Watchmen   http://bereanwatchmen.com/
- Bible Prophecy Today   bible-prophecy-today.blogspot.com/
- Friends of Israel   www.foi.org
- Grace to You   www.gty.org
- Grant Jeffrey Ministries   www.grantjeffrey.com/
- Koinonia House   www.khouse.org/
- Lighthouse Trails   www.lighthousetrailsresearch.com
- PreTrib Rapture Research www.pre-trib.org/
- Prophecy Central   www.bible-prophecy.com/
- Prophecy in the News   www.prophecyinthenews.com/
- Prophecy Today   www.prophecytoday.com/
- Rapture Ready   www.raptureme.com/
- Rapture Research Website www.pretribulationrapture.com/
- Rightly Dividing   www.righly-dividing.com
- Study-Grow-Know   www.studygrowknow.com
- Thomas Ice Writings   www.raptureme.com/ttcol.html
- Tyndale Theological Seminary   www.tyndale.edu

www.ingramcontent.com/pod-product-compliance
Lightning Source LLC
LaVergne TN
LVHW081353060426
835510LV00013B/1793